My Bible Diaries

Enlarge the Place of Your Tent
Isaiah 54 Blessings

Tarshish Productions
Elkhart, Indiana

Linda C. Newberry

Published by Tarshish Productions, 1933 N Stone Maple Lane, Elkhart, Indiana 46514.

Unless otherwise noted, Scripture quotations are taken from the King James Bible.

References to Strong's Concordance are taken from the Strong's Exhaustive Concordance in both book and electronic form.

Dictionary definitions mentioned are from Webster's (various editions), MacMillan and WordNet online Dictionary's

ISBN-10: 0976964031
ISBN-13: 978-0-9769640-3-2

www.lindacnewberry.com
Printed in the United States of America

Table of Contents

Acknowledgements

Thank you to the group of business associates, friends and family who have been a part of my weekday Bible study email. I have had many emails over the last several months telling me that in one way or another these word studies of verses have helped you to understand His meaning better, or that something in the study or prayer has hit a particular chord in whatever your current circumstance was, or just thanking me for opening this weekday study to you. Prior to the email I did my study in the form of journaling. This email started by sending off one of my daily studies as something to help a couple of my associates and now has morphed into something much larger.

What you may not know is the blessing it has been to me to be able to have a structured daily responsibility in providing these expanded verses, my musings and then a prayer to open the day. After spending well over the normal 40-50 hours a week during a 40+ year career and then being side-lined with physical difficulties, it has been a healing balm for me to know in a very real way that it is still possible to be effective and useful to people in my circle.

Thank you from the bottom of my heart.

Introduction

Welcome to My Bible Diaries!

Studying extensively is something I have done from almost my first moment as a Christian. My life was about as messy as it could get. Years of not understanding who I was or who I belonged to, created many wrong thought processes and thereby, speech patterns and actions that weren't worthy of a child of God.

One of the first gifts God gave me was an understanding that I needed more, a lot more, wisdom….and a hunger to find it. I was without work then, and I was offered a temporary position for several months. I was able to complete the work necessary within two to three hours but they still needed me there to answer the phones for the rest of the day. I asked if it would be okay to study my Bible during those five to six hours per day as long as I didn't let the reception duties slide and they happily agreed. Interesting, to say the least, considering they were not openly Christian folks. Thank you God!

There were other situations that engrained in me the need to study as a daily habit. The study convinced me of the importance of focused thinking and changing my speech patterns to include confessing right words. This carried through even when I worked full-time (although in-depth scripture study was a bit more sporadic), this study continued on a weekly basis.

I have been doing this in excess of twenty years now and continue to find new and exciting nuggets of God's gold. Recently I have had some physical issues that have brought me home from corporate America. I did not want to sit and wallow, which is especially easy to do when your body doesn't feel well. I wanted to continue to be of use. Although I was close to retirement age, it was still several years off. As much as we all talk about how great it will be once we aren't working, all people who go from 150 mph in the corporate setting to 1-10 mph find themselves wrestling with many questions about their new relevance in life and to humanity.

Relevance at work, in your position is easy to gage. Corporations are centered in measurable results and if you are good at what you do you have results that folks can see. However you come home after working for 40+ years and you find that most of your work friends don't call or come over. Some are uncomfortable. They don't know what to say. It becomes necessary to actively plan this new existence. You quickly find that you are and probably have been all along, responsible for finding your relevance while in my case caring for my body....and in your case caring for your family or career or when you are done with your career, the massive change from a 40+ hour week to the new frightening and exciting phase of retirement.

Healing takes time. In this situation a lot more time than I have wanted. Two to three hours of what I now call up time is what I have to offer, however my ability to do much physically is still severely limited. Setting aside upset about my external circumstance and choosing to look at this differently was important for me to move ahead.

One day a particular study I was working on had some nuggets I thought a couple of my friends could use to brighten their day. Their response was positive. So as I reached out to family/friends and ex-coworkers and associates over the next few months, I began to ask if they would be interested in joining our little weekday business person's study. Week by week the list grew. This weekday Bible study email has now turned into blog posts. This has become an avenue for me to keep in touch with many of my business associates, friends and now new followers and Facebook fans.

Neither you nor I will ever be at a point in our development to set aside study. The studies in this collection are meant to give you food for thought. They are not meant for full explanation and frankly, if I were to study them over again today there would be new nuggets that would come out. When you see the definitions and the verse, you will see more than what his written. You should expect that. It is one of the beauties of God's word. Depending on the time of life and things you are dealing with, different aspects of the verse will show itself.

These are verses or series of verses that have been used in my own life as confessions to change my circumstances, bringing my life to more closely resemble the life God had planned out for me. He paints vivid pictures of our health, our relationships (with Him and with others), our spiritual and emotional being, our social standing, our political leanings and….our life work, financial and material status. My hope is that you will find in these studies the reason and means to stand firm until you see change into that God vision designed just for you. These are studies that can and should be read over and over, used in Bible studies and mulled over in prayer time….this is not a one show pony.

The layout for the study starts with the chosen verse showing in parentheses the key definitions from the Strong's Concordance and/or extended definitions from the dictionary when needed; next my study and prayer for your day; finally you will find the full Strong's definition, followed by any root words associated with the word studied. The reason I am showing you these is that as I continue to be astounded at some of these definitions, I expect that you will be also. I do not want you to think I am just making this stuff up. That's how good it is!

You may ask, 'How can you promote this when you have a real and present health need yourself?' My answer is that my belief in healing is no less now than before I became afflicted, and I need these words more now than ever. I will continue to read and study....become more focused in my thinking and speech no matter what seems to be going on around me. I am not done yet! And neither are you!

Enjoy these studies and please feel free to contact us at info@lindacnewberry.com

We look forward to hearing from you.

CHAPTER 1

Life is a Paradox

Isaiah 54:1 (KJV)

1 Sing (*make joyful noise, triumph*), O barren (*male or female, sterile, hamstrung [make ineffective or powerless], to exterminate [destroy completely, as if down to the roots], pluck up*), thou that didst not bear (*to bear young, to show lineage [inherited properties shared with others of your bloodline, the descendants of one individual]*, to act as a midwife [*a woman skilled in aiding the delivery of babies*]); break forth into singing, and cry aloud, thou that didst not travail with child: for more are the children of the desolate than the children of the married wife, saith the LORD.

This is one of my favorite chapters in the Bible. We will take our time here and see what these word definitions reveal to us. We will see that, as always, there is the spiritual side of the lesson and the material side of the lesson as well.

We start this chapter out with the back drop of the foretelling the work that Jesus (the Christ, the Anointed Savior) would do for the world in his death....justifying many, bearing their iniquities and making intercession for the transgressors. Isaiah 53 says 'he will divide the spoil with the strong'. Isaiah 54 starts out talking about those that appear to be in a weakened state, but in the end come out on top. The words of this chapter fulfill the statement from Isaiah 53. He uses as analogy the idea of a woman who has never been able to have children and infers the emotional pain that goes along with that affliction.

In this time in history strong feelings of failure and disgrace accompanied not being able to give her husband children. After all this was the woman's role in fulfilling God's first directive to 'be fruitful and multiply'. The personal desire to be the vessel through which the next generation would be birthed and in that act complete this command was a driving force.

Imagine the emotional pain of being considered broken, unable to perform as society expected. Superstitious or mean spirited people would whisper behind your back that it is because your life was cursed, not favored by God, or possibly because you had some hidden sin that was at the bottom of this physical malfunction.

This chapter starts out saying that the weak are now strong. The instruction for those who did not bear....those who were barren was to make joyful noises, songs of triumph. Of course this can be those who are physically unable to have children, whether man or woman. But I feel that this goes much deeper.

His word calls the Church his bride and later in this chapter you will see the theme of the words here being pointed at women. However both men and women make up the Church, therefore these words will be equally relevant to both sexes. Today we have put to bullet point the individual Strong's and dictionary definitions of the words 'barren' and 'not bear'. Look at these and see if they apply to any area of your life:

> Male or female

> Sterile - someone who is sterile is not able to produce children; not very interesting and lacks fun and enjoyment; deficient in originality or creativity; lacking powers of invention

> Hamstrung - prevented from doing what you want to do; cripple by cutting the hamstring; make ineffective or powerless

> Exterminate - destroy completely, as if down to the roots

> Pluck up - to take someone quickly from a particular place or situation; pull lightly but sharply

> Uproot - to force someone out of the place where they live

> Beget – make children

> Show lineage – inherited properties shared with others of your bloodline; the descendants of one individual

> Act as midwife - a woman skilled in aiding the delivery of babies

Good morning, Father. Thank you for lighting a fire under us to rejoice and show joy outwardly even during those times when it doesn't look like we are producing the fruit you have commanded we produce. This is a part of the paradox often found when we look at your instruction to us. 'Let the weak say I am strong', 'Let the poor say I am rich'. We feel some of these defining words at one point or another in our lives; hamstrung, ineffective and powerless, uprooted, lacking enjoyment, no originality or creativity. Yet, you tell us in these words there is hope. Thank you for hope generated by our acts of obedience. When we speak against any negative circumstance, war against inward thoughts or words spoken over us by, and stand against situations that run contrary to your promise for us....when we sing songs of sunshine and happiness in a dark hour....we create an environment for seeds of hope to become stronger and stronger. Faith and hope generate an opening through which we begin to see your favor and grace become physically apparent. Results develop in front of our eyes. Thank you so much for renewed ability to receive your favor through all your various avenues. And Father the more we receive, the more we are able to pass on to others. We praise and thank you for your love, in Jesus' name....Amen!

Definitions for today's study:

Sing - a primitive root; properly **to creak** (or emit a stridulous sound), i.e. **to shout (usually for joy)** :- aloud for joy, cry out, **be joyful**, (greatly, make to) **rejoice**, (cause to) shout (for joy), (cause to) sing (aloud, for joy, out), **triumph**.

Barren - from <H6131> (`aqar); **sterile** (as if **extirpated in the generative organs**) :- **(× male or female) barren** (woman); a primitive root; to pluck up (especially by the roots); specifically to **hamstring [make ineffective or powerless]**; figurative **to exterminate** :- dig down, hough, **pluck up, root up**.

Bear - a primitive root; **to bear young**; causative to beget; to **act as midwife**; specifically **to show lineage [inherited properties shared with others of your bloodline, the descendants of one individual]**

CHAPTER 2

A Gleam in Your Eye,
A Song on Your Lips

Isaiah 54:1 (KJV)

1 Sing (*make joyful noise, triumph*), O barren, thou that didst not bear; break forth into singing, and cry aloud (*to gleam [an appearance of reflected light]*), thou that didst not travail with child: for more (*abundant in quantity, size, age, number, rank and quality; increase, multiply to the myriad, ten thousands, plenteous*) are the children (*a son, builder of the family name; to build either figuratively or literally; and in a wide sense-relationship, including grandson, subject, nation, quality or condition*) of the desolate than the children of the married wife, saith the LORD.

We are being asked to make an outward show of excitement, joy and triumph in the face of current or previous failure. This could be failure of your body as it is in this example. Or it could be that you have not handled your affairs (in your relationships, work or finances) very effectively to this point in life.

Perhaps you have felt a victim most of your life and have an inner knowing that there is something greater out there for you. Maybe you have been abandoned by those you were supposed to be able to trust or have been betrayed by your spouse or a business partner.

Could it be that you never felt like you had a real home, you moved around a lot and just as you were getting to feel comfortable you were plucked up and set in an unfamiliar setting....giving the sense of no continuity and/or always having to start all over again. Have you felt like the creativity has been drained out of you by consistently being told that you have to think and speak and act a certain way....or that your achievements are something to be hidden to save a non-achiever's feelings.

Have you tried and tried to get an idea off the ground and haven't yet seen the fruit of all your efforts? Well, all of these scenarios and many I've not mentioned could be set at and substituted at the first part of this verse. These kinds of life issues affect us in varying degrees throughout our lives. Unfortunately too many get bogged down by these and get stuck in the negative thought processes that can be developed during these times.

God's solution for this is to sing, to shout, and to have a gleam in your eye reflecting the joy in your heart. Why would you do this? How can you do this when you feel like you have been tackled by a 220lb linebacker? These are just the times when it is so necessary for us to understand the promises of God.

If we have not sought the kingdom of God and his righteousness, we have no idea what it is that we are supposed to expect from life. That is why teachings are so important. That is why I give you definitions to the words, because it is not enough for you to believe what I am saying about a passage....but that you can see where I have come up with my understanding.

The definitions placed at the end of our studies are for you to be able to search out the additional truths as they pertain to your life and not solely depend on what I or any other teacher, preacher or evangelist is telling you. This instruction to act with enthusiasm in the face of contrary situations is for a reason. God's desired end for us is to have us walking in victory, not just talking victory.

As we are continually reminded, words and actions come before the result.....and the result is that those who have not born, those who have been barren will have more children than the married wife. In the natural, a woman will have what, maybe 1 to 6 children normally?

Looking at this from a literal point of view, this is telling us that the woman without biological children can have far more than the size of a normal family by the influence she has over children of family member and other children or adults in her community. But, the figurative concept doesn't end there. We will explore that further in the next chapter.

Good morning, Father. Thank you for this seed of hope and our exercise of faith....that whatever area of life we have seen barrenness, better things are in our futures. Thank you for opening our eyes to the idea that even the saddest of times in our lives will be used to not only bring us increase, but will be able to be used to positively influence the people you bring us into contact with....that they will draw strength from us to move forward in their lives and that through these multiplying relationships the world will be made a better place. Thank you for grace that you use to bring us out of any funk created by these situations, give us the desire to want to move from victim to victor, and from follower to influencer in our circles. We thank you for unprecedented favor being poured into our lives. In Jesus name we praise and thank you....Amen!

Definitions for today's study:

Sing - a primitive root; properly **to creak** (or emit a stridulous sound), i.e. **to shout (usually for joy)** :- aloud for joy, cry out, **be joyful**, (greatly, make to) **rejoice**, (cause to) shout (for joy), (cause to) sing (aloud, for joy, out), **triumph**.

Barren - from <H6131> (`aqar); **sterile** (as if **extirpated in the generative organs**) :- **(× male or female) barren** (woman); a primitive root; to pluck up (especially by the roots); specifically to **hamstring [make ineffective or powerless]**; figurative **to exterminate** :- dig down, hough, **pluck up**, **root up**.

Bear - a primitive root; **to bear young**; causative to beget; to **act as midwife**; specifically **to show lineage [inherited properties shared with others of your bloodline, the descendants of one individual]**

Break forth - a primitive root; to **break out (in joyful sound)** :- **break (forth, forth into joy)**, make a loud noise.

Singing - from <H7442> (ranan); properly **a creaking (or shrill sound)**, i.e. shout (of joy or grief) :- cry, gladness, joy, proclamation, rejoicing, shouting, sing (-ing), triumph; a primitive root; properly to creak (or emit a stridulous sound), i.e. to shout (usually for joy) :- aloud for joy, cry out, be joyful, (greatly, make to) rejoice, (cause to) shout (for joy), (cause to) sing (aloud, for joy, out), triumph.

Cry aloud - a primitive root; **to gleam [an appearance of reflected light]**, i.e. (figurative) **be cheerful**; by transformation **to sound clear** (of various animal or human expressions) :- bellow, cry aloud (out), lift up, neigh, rejoice, make to shine, shout.

Travail with child - or chiyl, kheel; a primitive root; **properly to twist or whirl** (in a circular or spiral manner), i.e. (specific) to dance, **to writhe in pain (especially of parturition)** or fear; figurative to wait, to pervert :- bear, (make to) bring forth, (make to) calve, dance, drive away, fall grievously (with pain), fear, form, great, grieve, (be) grievous, hope, look, make, be in pain, be much (sore) pained, rest, shake, shapen, (be) sorrow (-ful), stay, tarry, travail (with pain), tremble, trust, wait carefully (patiently), be wounded.

For more - by contracted from <H7231> (rabab); **abundant (in quantity, size, age, number, rank, quality)** :- (in) **abound** (-undance, -ant, -antly), captain, elder, enough, **exceedingly, full, great** (-ly, man, one), increase, long (enough, [time]), (do, have) many (-ifold, things, a time), ([ship-]) master, mighty, more, **(too, very) much, multiply** (-tude), officer, often [-times], **plenteous**, populous, prince, process [of time], suffice (-ient); a primitive root; properly to cast together [compare <H7241> (rabiyb)], i.e. **increase**, especially in number; also (as denominative from <H7233> (rebabah)) **to multiply by the myriad** :- increase, be many (-ifold), be more, multiply, **ten thousands**.

Are the children - from <H1129> (banah); **a son (as a builder of the family name), in the widest sense (of literal and figurative relationship, including grandson, subject, nation, quality or condition, etc**.; a primitive root; **to build (literal and figurative)** :- (begin to) build (-er), obtain children, **make**, repair, set (up), × surely.

Of the desolate - a primitive root; **to stun (or intransitive grow numb)**, i.e. **devastate** or (figurative) **stupefy** (both usually in a passive sense) :- make amazed, **be astonied (filled with the emotional impact of overwhelming surprise or shock)**, (be an) astonish (-ment), (be, bring into, unto, lay, lie, make) **desolate [completely empty, no people or pleasant features; crushed by grief; devastated, ravaged, uninhabitable, providing no shelter or sustenance, leaving someone who needs you or counts on you hanging in the lurch]**(-ion, places), **be destitute (with no**

money or possessions, poor enough to need help from others), **destroy (damage something so severely that it no longer exists and can never return to its normal state, defeat an opponent completely)** (self), (lay, lie, make) **waste (the failure to use something valuable in an effective way, so that it does not produce the benefits that it could; a situation in which time, money, or energy is used without bringing any useful result; lose vigor, health, or flesh, as through grief; get rid of (someone who may be a threat) by killing)**, **wonder (place in doubt or express doubtful speculation)**

Of the married wife - a primitive root; to be master; hence (as denominative from <H1167> (ba`al)) to marry :- have dominion (over), be husband, marry (-ried, × wife); from <H1166> (ba`al); a master; hence a husband, or (figurative) owner (often used with another noun in modifications of this latter sense) :- + archer, + babbler, + bird, captain, chief man, + confederate, + have to do, + dreamer, those to whom it is due, + furious, those that are given to it, great, + hairy, he that hath it, have, + horseman, husband, lord, **man**, **+ married**, master, **person**, + sworn, they of.

Saith - a primitive root; **to say** (used with great latitude) :- answer, appoint, **avouch [admit openly and bluntly; make no bones about]**, bid, boast self, call, **certify**, challenge, charge, + (at the, give) command (-ment), commune, consider, declare, **demand**, × **desire**, **determine**, × expressly, × indeed, × **intend**, name, × plainly, **promise**, publish, report, **require**, say, speak (against, of), × still, × suppose, talk, tell, term, × that is, × think, use [speech], utter, × verily, × yet

The Lord - from <H1961> (hayah); (the) self-Existent or Eternal; **Jehovah,** Jewish national name of God :- Jehovah, the Lord. Compare <H3050> (Yahh), <H3069> (Yehovih); a primitive root [compare <H1933> (hava')]; to exist, i.e. be or become, come to pass (always emphatic, and not a mere copula or auxiliary) :- beacon, × altogether, be (-come, accomplished, committed, like), break, cause, come (to pass), do, faint, fall, + follow, happen, × have, last, pertain, quit (one-) self, require, × use.

CHAPTER 3

Rebound, Restoration & Strength

Isaiah 54:1 (KJV)

1 Sing, O barren, thou that didst not bear; break forth into singing, and cry aloud, thou that didst not travail with child: for more (*abundant in quantity, size, age, number, rank and quality; increase, multiply to the myriad, ten thousands, plenteous*) are the children (*a son, builder of the family name; to build either figuratively or literally; and in a wide sense-relationship, including grandson, subject, nation, quality or condition*) of the desolate than the children of the married wife, saith the LORD.

The idea of 'married wife' seems to infer a person of completed state. She has a husband. He is friend, companion, collaborator, lover, and provider....father of her children. They have come together and have a life plan. In this time in history a married woman with children was a successful woman.

This verse also differentiates between this state of emotional, spiritual, material and physical wholeness (so to speak) with that of a desolate person.

The desolate person is described as someone who has been stunned, someone who has grown numb; a person who is astonished, overwhelmed with shock or surprise; completely empty, crushed by grief, ravaged; no money or possessions; damaged beyond repair; wasted, or failure to be use something valuable in an effective way, producing no benefit.

This pretty well describes how we have been left after one or more bad experiences in life. What affects one person adversely another might take with ease and vice versa. One person may look at being fired from a position as an open door of opportunity, while another may take that as a blow to their life they may never recover from....in essence being desolated by the firing.

This verse is promising us something great to look forward to. It points to increase in our lives; abundance in quantity, size, age, number, rank and quality. It points to an unlimited increase; multiplying to the myriad (a large indefinite number)...tens of thousands. And although 'children' can mean our little ones, the strength of your family....or as they would have said in Biblical time 'arrows in your quiver', this word can mean much more.

This Hebrew word can mean to build. When you build something all or some of these aspects can be included; to develop; to increase in size and number; to order, supervise or finance construction; establish something from the abstract (an idea); give form to something according to a plan; to bolster or strengthen.

We are to be tenacious in our endeavors, knowing that we will encounter obstacles and may even get knocked down a few times before we see this promised success. We need to do our best to keep our eyes on our life and our prize. Comparing yourself to someone who may look like this 'married wife' will get you sidetracked and serve no concrete purpose. Besides that, just because someone looks as though they have it all (or always have had) there is no way for you to know the depths of their spirit and soul....and therefore no way to know what struggles they have faced. We are just not that different from one another in experiences and if we get to know that person we will find many similarities.

Good morning, Father. Thank you for this promise of rebound, restoration, and strength. Thank you for understanding that when we look at the words you have so carefully chosen for these instructions, more is opened to us than just the narrow translation we see on the page. When we understand the definitions of the words we see, we can know that we are not adding to or subtracting from your word....but instead, utilizing the full strength of the words you have selected. To do less is to not fully receive from you. Thank you for this verse that has uses 'saith the Lord'. We know from previous study that 'avouch' is part of its meaning, and avouch means to admit openly and bluntly, making no bones about it. Basically we can take this to the bank. We choose to receive this from you in Jesus name....Amen!

Definitions for today's study:
For more - by contracted from <H7231> (rabab); **abundant (in quantity, size, age, number, rank, quality)** :- (in) **abound** (-undance, -ant, -antly), captain, elder, enough, **exceedingly, full, great** (-ly, man, one), increase, long (enough, [time]), (do, have) many (-ifold, things, a time), ([ship-]) master, mighty, more, **(too, very) much, multiply** (-tude), officer, often [-times], **plenteous**, populous, prince, process [of time], suffice (-ient); a

primitive root; properly to cast together [compare <H7241> (rabiyb)], i.e. **increase**, especially in number; also (as denominative from <H7233> (rebabah)) **to multiply by the myriad** :- increase, be many (-ifold), be more, multiply, **ten thousands**.

Are the children - from <H1129> (banah); **a son (as a builder of the family name), in the widest sense (of literal and figurative relationship, including grandson, subject, nation, quality or condition, etc**.; a primitive root; **to build (literal and figurative)** :- (begin to) build (-er), obtain children, **make**, repair, set (up), × surely.

Of the desolate - a primitive root; **to stun (or intransitive grow numb)**, i.e. **devastate** or (figurative) **stupefy** (both usually in a passive sense) :- make amazed, **be astonied (filled with the emotional impact of overwhelming surprise or shock**), (be an) astonish (-ment), (be, bring into, unto, lay, lie, make) **desolate [completely empty, no people or pleasant features; crushed by grief; devastated, ravaged, uninhabitable, providing no shelter or sustenance, leaving someone who needs you or counts on you hanging in the lurch)**(-ion, places), **be destitute (with no money or possessions, poor enough to need help from others), destroy (damage something so severely that it no longer exists and can never return to its normal state, defeat an opponent completely)** (self), (lay, lie, make) **waste (the failure to use something valuable in an effective way, so that it does not produce the benefits that it could; a situation in which time, money, or energy is used without bringing any useful result; lose vigor, health, or flesh, as through grief; get rid of (someone who may be a threat) by killing), wonder (place in doubt or express doubtful speculation)**

Saith - a primitive root; **to say** (used with great latitude) :- answer, appoint, **avouch [admit openly and bluntly; make no bones about]**, bid, boast self, call, **certify**, challenge, charge, + (at the, give) command (-ment), commune, consider, declare, **demand**, × **desire**, **determine**, × expressly, × indeed, × **intend**, name, × plainly, **promise**, publish, report, **require**, say, speak (against, of), × still, × suppose, talk, tell, term, × that is, × think, use [speech], utter, × verily, × yet

CHAPTER 4

Conspicuously Seen

Isaiah 54:2 (KJV)

2 Enlarge (*to broaden, make large, make room, open wide*) the place (*a standing, a spot, locality, condition of body or mind*) of thy tent (*clearly conspicuous from a distance, covering, to be clear*), and let them stretch forth (*spread out, bend away*) the curtains (*hanging as tremulous, be broken up with violent action*) of thine habitations (*residence, to reside or permanently stay*): spare (*restrain, refrain, refuse*) not, lengthen (*draw out*) thy cords (*of a tent, or string of a bow, to jut over or exceed, by impl. to excel*), and strengthen (*to fasten upon, to seize, be strong*) thy stakes (*to tin through or fast, peg, nail*);

With the idea in mind that we will have more children (literally and figuratively), the next instruction is that we have more space for them to grow in. The square footage requirement for newlyweds is much less than when they begin to add children to the family. You find the area that once was more than enough space has become cramped and crowded when children arrive.

He is saying make room for an expansion in your life.

Open wide to seeing your standing (business and community status, social reputation) develop into something much bigger than you have seen or allowed in the past. This may take a paradigm shift. You may need to completely rethink who you are and where you are going. This first takes a change of mind.

What I really thought was very cool is that the word 'tent' isn't just about a covering to keep the elements out. It is not just some little camping tent or a lean-to. The description is something that can be conspicuously seen from a distance. Being conspicuous is being very noticeable or easy to see, especially because of being unusual or different; very great; obvious to the eye or mind; in a manner tending to attract attention; in a prominent way.

Many of us grew up attempting to be anything but conspicuous, perhaps having a spotlight shined on you was too uncomfortable. Yet it is something that most of us have also desired at some level, but fear has held us back. We want to be noticed and evidently….so does God!

This goes on to tell us to spread out, stretch forth or even one of the definitions is to let down (take aside) our curtains. Curtains cover openings, separate one room from another, can be a barrier to communication, keep prying eyes out and light from coming in, and are pulled up or aside when a performance is about to begin. Is He telling us to get ready for center stage?

This is our habitation, that place we will permanently stay. We are not to hold back, stop taking these steps or plant our feet and refuse to do this. Instead the excess material of this super-sized tent will require longer and stronger cords and tent stakes to stabilize the structure and act as the foundation that will keep it standing. A strong foundation makes it easier to be courageous and free to risk taking our rightful place, the place God has waiting for us. Taking that place confidently is not ego or lack of humility, but instead is the most humble position for us to be in. Confidence is often mistaken for a lack of humility....but it is not so.

Good morning, Father. Thank you for showing us your desire for us. We were not meant to be inconspicuous in our time, but instead are meant to use our talent and skills to grow our ideas and help other people develop theirs. Religion has often taught us that for us to be in the spotlight is ego based behavior, but your word tells us you want us in the middle of and at the head of government, companies, churches and families. As in Moses time we find that we are heads over people; rulers of thousands, rulers of hundreds, rulers of fifties, and rulers of tens; each of us with our area of influence, our own skill sets and talents to serve. As we prepare for increase, bring us the individual knowledge we will need to strengthen our foundation and the wisdom to know how to put the information to proper use. Thank you for favor shown to us in all quarters, and for giving us ample opportunity to show grace and favor to those we come into contact with. In Jesus name we praise and thank you....Amen!

Definitions for today's study:
Enlarge - a primitive root; **to broaden** (intransitive or transitive, literal or figurative) :- be an en- **(make) large** (-ing), **make room**, make **(open) wide**.
Place - or maqom, maw-kome'; also (feminine) meqowmah, mek-o-mah'; or meqomah, mek-o-mah'; from <H6965> (quwm);

properly **a standing**, i.e. **a spot**; but **used widely of a locality** (general or specific); also (figurative) of **a condition (of body or mind)** :- country, × home, × open, place, room, space, × whither [-soever]; a primitive root; **to rise** (in various applications, literal, figurative, intensive and causative) :- abide, **accomplish**, × **be clearer**, confirm, continue, decree, × be dim, endure, × enemy, enjoin, get up, make good, help, hold, (help to) lift up (again), make, × but newly, ordain, perform, pitch, raise (up), rear (up), remain, (a-) rise (up) (again, against), rouse up, set (up), (e-) stablish, (make to) stand (up), stir up, **strengthen**, **succeed**, (as-, make) sure (-ly), (be) up (-hold, -rising)

Tent - from <H166> ('ahal); a **tent (as clearly conspicuous from a distance)** :- **covering**, (dwelling) (place), home, tabernacle, tent; a primitive root; **to be clear** :- shine.

Stretch forth - a primitive root; **to stretch or spread out**; by implication **to bend away (including moral deflection)**; used in a great variety of application (as follows) :- + afternoon, apply, bow (down, -ing), carry aside, decline, deliver, extend, go down, be gone, incline, intend, lay, let down, offer, outstretched, overthrown, pervert, pitch, prolong, put away, shew, spread (out), stretch (forth, out), take (aside), turn (aside, away), wrest, cause to yield.

Curtains - from <H3415> (yara`); **a hanging (as tremulous)** :- curtain; a primitive root; properly to **be broken up (with any violent action)**, i.e. (figurative) to fear :- be grievous [only Isa. 15:4; the rest belong to <H7489> (ra`a`)].

Habitations - from <H7931> (shakan); **a residence** (including a shepherd's hut, the lair of animals, figurative the grave; also the Temple); specifically the Tabernacle (properly its wooden walls) :- dwelleth, dwelling (place), habitation, tabernacle, tent; a primitive root [apparently akin (by transmission) to <H7901> (shakab) through the idea of lodging; compare <H5531> (cikluwth), <H7925> (shakam)]; **to reside or permanently stay** (literal or figurative) :- abide, continue, (cause to, make to) **dwell** (-er), have habitation, inhabit, lay, place, (cause to) remain, **rest**, set (up)

Spare - a primitive root; **to restrain** or (reflexsive) **refrain**; by implication to **refuse**, spare, preserve; also (by interch. with <H2821> (chashak)) to observe :- assuage, × darken, forbear, hinder, hold back, keep (back), punish, refrain, reserve, spare, withhold;

Lengthen - a primitive root; to be (causative make) long (literal or figurative) :- defer, **draw out**, lengthen, (be, become, make, pro-) long, + (out-, over-) live, tarry (long).

Thy cords - from <H3498> (yathar); a cord (of a tent) [compare <H3499> (yether)] or the string (of a bow) :- cord, string; a primitive root; **to jut over or exceed; by implication to excel**; (intransitive) to remain or be left; causative to leave, cause to abound, preserve :- excel, leave (a remnant), left behind, too much, make plenteous, preserve, (be, let) remain (-der, -ing, -nant), reserve, residue, rest.

Strengthen - a primitive root; **to fasten upon**; hence **to seize, be strong (figurative courageous, causative strengthen, cure, help, repair, fortify)**, obstinate; to bind, restrain, conquer :- aid, amend, × calker, catch, cleave, confirm, be constant, constrain, continue, be of good (take) courage (-ous, -ly), encourage (self), be established, fasten, force, fortify, make hard, harden, help, (lay) hold (fast), lean, maintain, play the man, mend, become (wax) mighty, prevail, be recovered, repair, retain, seize, be (wax) sore, strengthen (self), be stout, be (make, shew, wax) strong (-er), be sure, take (hold), be urgent, behave self valiantly, withstand.

Stakes - from an unused root meaning **to pin through or fast**; **a peg** :- **nail**, paddle, pin, stake.

CHAPTER 5

It Will Definitely Happen

Isaiah 54:3 (KJV)

3 For thou shalt (*something will definitely happen*) break forth (*burst out, disperse, grow, increase*) on the right hand (*the stronger and more dexterous*) and on the left (*through the idea of a cover, assuming the shape of the object beneath*); and thy seed (*posterity, children, fruit, to fructify or make productive*) shall inherit (*take possession, driving out previous tenants and enjoy*) the Gentiles (*a foreign nation*), and make the desolate (*stunned, numbed, astonished*) cities (*a place guarded by a watch, to wake literally or figuratively*) to be inhabited (*to dwell and remain*).

By beginning right where you are….acting with a joyful attitude (which is an heart action, requiring physical response), speaking and/or singing happy triumphant songs and words (another physical action) and having a gleam in your eye that others can see, you step in line for better things happening in your life. Why? Because you see something now that others don't yet.

These actions require faith that they will work. The truth is when we first begin to do this we are stepping out on a

35

limb, we are staking claim and saying things will not remain as they seem to be now....and sometimes we just don't know it is true. We are choosing to take God at his word and this is hard considering the number of times we have been let down in the past.

It is important to remember that in any adverse situation our mind and heart may not want to act in faith but instead we choose obedience to the command from God. When we act in obedience, even if we are not fully convinced that the action requested/required will bring about the desirable results....these acts of obedience bolster our hope and build faith in the process.

In this verse, it says 'for you shall'. This means something will _definitely happen_. And what is that something? Increase will happen. Growth will happen. Your physical, material life will prove to be bursting at the seams. You now can begin to see the reason for preparation. You were asked to expand that tent and if you don't, what is coming will like attempting to put 10 pounds of gold nuggets in a 5 pound burlap bag.

It will not do what the Glad Force Flex bags do. Instead this burlap bag, this tent that once was capable of holding the contents of your life will be, definitely bursting at the seams. The contents of your life will increase on the right and left.

The right speaks of strength and getting stronger. The left speaks of covering, assuming the shape of the object underneath. What happens if you don't open your eyes and expand your vision, would the mention of the 'left' here mean that your expansion will be limited to that underlying smaller vision?

This verse tells us that our productivity will definitely take possession of the Gentiles (a foreign nation, from the prime root – mount up, be majestic, and/or increase). Our productivity makes us take possession of higher social or business or political standing, we take possession of the majestic show of His favor in our life and increase will be possessed by us. Our productivity will make these desolate places in our life wake up and come alive. Our dreams and visions that we have seen in our heart and mind will become inhabitable. They will become a place for us to dwell and remain.

Good morning, Father. Thank you for breaking this down for us. Your word provides us with the 'why' and the 'what'....the 'how', the 'when', the 'where' are secrets that will be unlocked when we are ready....when your timing is just right. Thank you for the promise that as we prepare for increase, it becomes that much closer to being seen in our lives, not only for our benefit....but for the benefit of those who see us and know there is something different about us. This difference will not only be the glitter of gold, but the gold will be that shiny object, so many think they are looking for....it will act as an attractor and give us more opportunity to give voice to our dependence on you. We understand that our preparation includes so many things; integrity, character, boundaries, money management, the ability to influence properly, and the desire to act out of love ....you have been schooling us. We ask for whatever correction is needed to bring us along. We know that we will not be perfect and will make mistakes, but you Father, will draw us back to the path. Thank you for enough schooling that once we conquer land we will not give it up to vice. Your grace and favor wrap us up in protection....and our gratitude make us desire even more to find someone to bless today. In Jesus' holy name, we praise and thank you....Amen!

Definitions for today's study:
Break forth - a primitive root; **to break out** (in many applications, direct and indirect, literal and figurative) :- × abroad, (make a) breach, break (away, down, -er, forth, in, up), **burst out**, come (spread) abroad, compel, **disperse**, **grow**, **increase**, open, **press**, scatter, urge.
Right hand - from <H3231> (yaman); the right hand or side (leg, eye) of a person or other object (as **the stronger and more dexterous**); locally, the south :- + left-handed, right (hand, side), south; a primitive root; to be (physical) right (i.e. firm); but used only as denominative from <H3225> (yamiyn) and transitive, to be right-handed or take the right-hand side :- go (turn) to (on, use) the right hand.
Left - or semo'l, sem-ole'; a primitive word [rather perhaps from the same as <H8071> (simlah) (by insertion of aleph) through the idea of wrapping up]; properly dark (as enveloped), i.e. the north; hence (by orientation) the left hand :- left (hand, side); perhaps by permutation for the feminine of <H5566> (cemel) **(through the idea of a cover assuming the shape of the object beneath)**; a dress, especially a mantle :- apparel, cloth (-es, -ing), garment, raiment. Compare <H8008> (salmah); or cemel, say'-mel; from an unused root meaning to resemble; a likeness :- figure, idol, image.
Seed - from <H2232> (zara`); seed; figurative **fruit**, plant, sowing-time, **posterity** :- × carnally, child, fruitful, seed (-time), sowing-time; a primitive root; to sow; figurative to disseminate, plant, **fructify [make productive]** :- bear, conceive seed, set with, sow (-er), **yield**.
Inherit - or yaresh, yaw-raysh'; a primitive root; **to occupy (by driving out previous tenants, and possessing in their place)**; by implication **to seize**, to rob, to inherit; also to expel, to impoverish, to ruin :- cast out, consume, destroy, disinherit,

dispossess, drive (-ing) out, **enjoy**, expel, × without fail, (give to, leave for) inherit (-ance, -or), + magistrate, be (make) poor, come to poverty, (give to, make to) possess, get (have) in **(take) possession**, seize upon, succeed, × utterly.

Gentiles - rarely (shortened) goy, go'-ee; apparently from the same root as <H1465> (gevah) (in the sense of massing); **a foreign nation**; hence a Gentile; also (figurative) a troop of animals, or a flight of locusts :- Gentile, heathen, nation, people; feminine of <H1460> (gev); the back, i.e. (by extension) the person :- body; from <H1342> (ga'ah) [corresponding to <H1354> (gab)]; the back; by analogy the middle :- + among, back, body; *a primitive root*; **to mount up**; hence in general to rise, (figurative) **be majestic** :- gloriously, grow up, **increase**, be risen, triumph.

Desolate - a primitive root; **to stun (or intransitive grow numb)**, i.e. **devastate** or (figurative) **stupefy** (both usually in a passive sense) :- make amazed, **be astonied (filled with the emotional impact of overwhelming surprise or shock**), (be an) astonish (-ment), (be, bring into, unto, lay, lie, make) **desolate [completely empty, no people or pleasant features; crushed by grief; devastated, ravaged, uninhabitable, providing no shelter or sustenance, leaving someone who needs you or counts on you hanging in the lurch)**(-ion, places), **be destitute (with no money or possessions, poor enough to need help from others)**, **destroy (damage something so severely that it no longer exists and can never return to its normal state, defeat an opponent completely)** (self), (lay, lie, make) **waste (the failure to use something valuable in an effective way, so that it does not produce the benefits that it could; a situation in which time, money, or energy is used without bringing any useful result; lose vigor, health, or flesh, as through grief; get rid of (someone who may be a threat) by killing)**, **wonder (place in doubt or express doubtful speculation)**

Cities - or (in the plural) ar, awr; or ayar, aw-yar'; (Judg. 10:4), from <H5782> (`uwr) **a city (a place guarded by waking or a watch)** in the widest sense (even of a mere encampment or

39

post) :- Ai [from margin], city, court [from margin], town; a primitive root [rather identical with <H5783> (`uwr) **through the idea of opening the eyes**]; **to wake (literal or figurative)** :- (a-) wake (-n, up), lift up (self), × master, raise (up), stir up (self).

Inhabited - a primitive root; properly **to sit down** (specifically as judge, in ambush, in quiet); by implication **to dwell, to remain**; causative **to settle**, to marry :- (make to) abide (-ing), continue, (cause to, make to) dwell (-ing), ease self, endure, establish, × fail, habitation, haunt, (make to) inhabit (-ant), make to keep [house], lurking, × marry (-ing), (bring again to) place, remain, return, seat, set (-tle), (down-) sit (-down, still, -ting down, -ting [place] -uate), take, tarry.

CHAPTER 6

Focus: Clouded Vision or Blue Skies

Isaiah 54:4 (KJV)

4 Fear not; for thou shalt not be ashamed (*paled-sick, shocked, worried; less impressive; not as good as*): neither be thou confounded (*wounded, taunted, insulted, perplexed by conflicting situations/statements, bewildered*); for thou shalt not be put to shame (*fail to meet hopes or expectations, disappointed, confused, criticized or reproached*): for thou shalt forget (*mislay, be oblivious by not noticing, or knowing about or fail to keep in mind*) the shame (*painful emotion of inadequacy or guilt, a state of dishonor*) of thy youth (*adolescence, vigor, veiled from sight, secret things*), and shalt not remember (*mark to be recognized, mention, be mindful of, recount, think on*) the reproach (*rude expressions intended to offend or hurt, harsh language/treatment arising from haughtiness and contempt*) of thy widowhood (*bereavement, discarded, forsaken*) any more.

In the previous verses we are told to sing and speak and act with joy....in triumph no matter what we may see in our circumstances. The end result was 'for you shall', meaning something *will definitely happen*. But it also promises the negative things you will not be burdened with. The promise is 'for you shall not', meaning these things *will definitely not happen*. Much of the pain experienced in life is emotional and mental pain….this type of pain is much more difficult to overcome than physical pain.

The thing is that the more time we spend in gaining understanding of all the good God has for us, the more these negative thoughts and feelings dissipate….literally these old feelings and thoughts become less strong until they fade away altogether. This is saying that *we will* definitely *not*:

- **Be ashamed**

  - ➢ paled because of sickness, shock or worry

  - ➢ be less impressive, important, serious or not as good when compared with someone or something similar

  - ➢ confused by guilt

  - ➢ conviction or conscious of wrong action or impropriety

  - ➢ disappointed or delayed

- **Confounded**

  - ➢ To wound

  - ➢ To taunt or insult

  - ➢ Blush

  - ➢ Perplexed by conflicting situations or statement

> Filled with bewilderment

- **Shamed**

  > The idea of being detected

  > Fail to meet hopes or expectations

  > Brought to confusion

If you look at this list, these are many of the things that keep us stuck in that place of doing nothing. Instead of looking to the future (and as Jeremiah 29:11 states we can't fully know what God has in store for us), we allow the mistakes and improprieties of the past cloud our vision of what can be.

Memories of past failures, youthful foolishness and indiscretion can be debilitating if we do not put them in their place. These debilitating thoughts can keep us in a place of incorrectly believing that we don't measure up, and never will to the achievements of others. Those others could be people from our own family line that we are internally competing with or the person in the next cubicle at work.

If we have been able to step out in the direction of the dream God placed in our heart, we can run into the problem of temporary failure and become disappointed at the length of time it is taking to reach our goal. Succumbing to these unproductive thoughts can make us slow down or quit moving forward at all.

In some cases it is the words of others that have kept us down. We want to be loved and accepted by others and that doesn't always happen. As we become more mature we learn the benefit of boundaries and the power of choosing our associates well. Believe it or not there will come a time when your circle of friends is like a fortress to you and with their support the words of others will not have the sting they once did.

Whatever the mental or emotional obstacle, it is not bigger than God and the amazing plan he has for us.

His second promise in this verse is that we will forget any painful emotion of inadequacy or guilt, any state of dishonor....those secret things from our past. We won't notice or be mindful of the rude things said about us that were meant to offend or hurt us; we won't think about or recount bad treatment from haughty people....those who have considered themselves so much better than they saw us. We won't even mention those times in our lives when we were forsaken or when we felt discarded by others.

Two things come to mind about these promises. One is that every person on the face of the planet experiences these types of feelings and experiences whether they show it on the outside or not. If this were not the case, it would not be mentioned here. And secondly, what God promises is such an erasure, such an expunging of the hurt of the situation that it no longer impedes our progress and His free flow of blessing to our lives.

Strangely, we remember the lesson of the situation. However it contains little to none of the sting it once carried. Once the sting is removed, the lesson is not only used as a building block of our future but also can and should be used to help someone through a hard time.

Good morning, Father. Thank you for not only the promise but the reality of your love removing the hidden pain of guilt and shame that we each have experienced in this life. Thank you for carrying the pain of failure and inadequate feelings....for building within us a confidence that cannot be shaken when others attack us in the course of our day to day life. Thank you for the understanding that as we speak these things into the atmosphere they are doing their work and we will see their result come to fruition. Thank you for wisdom to take the next right step, for vision for expansion, for grace that overcomes obstacles, and favor that paves the way. Thank you for those we are in partnership with, for people who desire to see the best for us and for divine connections that you have lined up for us in the days ahead. We ask for eyes to see the need around us, the desire to serve and the discernment to pick and choose wisely. In Jesus' holy name, we praise and thank you....Amen!

Definitions for today's study:

Fear - a primitive root; **to fear**; moral **to revere**; causative **to frighten** :- affright, **be (make) afraid**, dread (-ful), (put in) fear (-ful, -fully, -ing), (be had in) reverence (-end), × see, terrible (act, -ness, thing).

Ashamed - a primitive root; properly **to pale [face pales, their skin becomes lighter because they are sick, shocked, or worried, less impressive, important, serious or not as good as before or when compared with someone or something similar]**, i.e. by implication to be ashamed [abashed or confused by guilt, or a conviction or consciousness of some wrong action or impropriety]; also (by implication) **to be disappointed, or delayed** :- (be, make, bring to, cause, put to, with, a-) shame (-d), be (put to) confounded (-fusion), become dry, delay, be long.

Confounded - a primitive root; properly **to wound**; but only figurative, **to taunt or insult** :- be (make) ashamed, **blush**, **be confounded [perplexed by many conflicting situations or statements; filled with bewilderment]**, **be put to confusion**, hurt, reproach, (do, put to) shame.

Shame - a primitive root [perhaps rather the same as <H2658> (chaphar) through the idea of detection]; to blush; figurative to be ashamed, **disappointed [fail to meet the hopes or expectations of];** causative to shame, reproach :- be ashamed, be confounded, **be brought to confusion (unto shame)**, come (be put to) shame, bring **reproach [to criticize someone and feel disappointed with them for something they have done]**; a primitive root; properly to pry into; by implication to delve, to explore :- dig, paw, search out, seek.

Forget - or shakeach, shaw-kay'-akh; a primitive root; **to mislay [place (something) where one cannot find it again]**, i.e. **to be oblivious of [not noticing, or knowing about, failing to keep in mind]**, from want of memory or attention :- × at all, (cause to) forget.

Shame - from <H954> (buwsh); **shame [a painful emotion resulting from an awareness of inadequacy or guilt, a state of dishonor, unfortunate development]** (the feeling and the condition, as well as its cause); by implication (specific) an idol :- ashamed, confusion, + greatly, (put to) shame (-ful thing); a primitive root; properly to pale, i.e. by implication to be ashamed; also (by implication) to be disappointed, or delayed :- (be, make, bring to, cause, put to, with, a-) shame (-d), be (put to) confounded (-fusion), become dry, delay, be long.

Youth - passive participle of <H5956> (`alam) in the denominative sense of <H5958> (`elem); (only in plural as abstract) **adolescence**; figurative **vigor** :- youth; a primitive root; **to veil from sight**, i.e. conceal (literal or figurative) :- × any ways, blind, dissembler, hide (self), **secret (thing)**; from <H5956> (`alam); properly something kept out of sight [compare <H5959> (`almah)], i.e. a lad :- young man, stripling.

Remember - a primitive root; properly **to mark (so as to be recognized)**, i.e. to remember; by implication **to mention**; also (as denominative from <H2145> (zakar)) to be male :- × burn [incense], × earnestly, be male, (make) mention (of), **be mindful**, **recount**, **record** (-er), remember, make to be remembered, bring (call, come, keep, put) to (in) remembrance, × still, **think on**, × well; from <H2142> (zakar); properly remembered, i.e. a male (of man or animals, as being the most noteworthy sex) :- × him, male, man (child, -kind).

Reproach - from <H2778> (charaph); **contumely [a rude expression intended to offend or hurt, harsh language or treatment arising from haughtiness and contempt]**, **disgrace**, the pudenda :- rebuke, reproach (-fully), shame; a primitive root; to pull off, i.e. (by implication) **to expose (as by stripping)**; specifically to **betroth (as if a surrender)**; figurative **to carp at**, i.e. defame; denominative (from <H2779> (choreph)) to spend the winter :- betroth, **blaspheme**, defy, jeopard, rail, reproach, upbraid; from <H2778> (charaph); properly the crop gathered, i.e. (by implication) the autumn (and winter) season; figurative ripeness of age :- cold, winter ([-house]), youth;.

Widowhood - feminine of <H488> ('alman); concrete **a widow**; abstract widowhood :- widow, widowhood; prolonged from <H481> ('alam) in the **sense of bereavement**; **discarded (as a divorced person)** :- **forsaken**; a primitive root; **to tie fast**; hence (of the mouth) to be tongue-tied :- bind, be dumb, put to silence.

CHAPTER 7

Puzzle Pieces & Royal Responsibility

Isaiah 54:5 (KJV)

5 For thy Maker (*to make, have the charge of, maintain, provide*) is thine husband (*married to you, to be master*); the LORD of hosts (*organized for war, like an army; a mass of persons or figurative things*) is his name; and thy Redeemer (*kinsman, and as such to buy back a relative's property, marry his widow, etc*) the Holy One of Israel; The God of the whole earth shall he be called.

As mentioned in the previous verse, we will definitely not remember the reproach of our widowhood anymore and will not be put to shame. The reason is stated in this verse.
It is because He is our Maker, husband, Lord of hosts, our Redeemer, the Holy One of Israel, and The God of the whole earth.

In the role of our Maker he did not only form us but also has specific responsibility to his creation, and that creation is us. We may not always think of God as having responsibility for us once we are here, but certainly the expansive definition of the word 'maker' makes us think a bit more deeply about it.

The creation is brought forth and then given or sold to the world for its purpose, by its creator or inventor. And who better to know the elements needed for repair and maintenance than the one who put it together?

God has designed us with a particular purpose in mind. Through our being the person he created we are used to pull other pieces of this earthly puzzle together. Our lives are locked in place with thousands of others to complete the picture at any given point in time.

Sometimes we see an opening in the picture and look at our shape and size and think we will fit into that 'slot', only to find that it is not an exact fit. But eventually we find that spot we were designed for and voila! Other pieces of the puzzle begin to fall into place. Without us and our usefulness there would be a hole in the finished picture of all of the lives we touch.

In the role of husband His responsibility is to provide for us and keep us safe and secure (guarding our hearts and minds and body). In the role of Lord of hosts (army, His angelic host), he provides us with protection from warring factions. Ephesians 6:10 tells us that our wars are not with flesh and blood but instead with powers and principalities.

Unfortunately for us, it feels like the person used in an attack against us is the one we should focus our negative attention on. Only through being taught otherwise and knowing this deep in our hearts can we stop ourselves from returning hateful actions and speech to those who act as an enemy. God and his host's focus are on the spiritual force behind the circumstances or person used to attack us and we need to unify with God in this line of focus.

In the role of Redeemer, he acts as they did in the days of old by paying our debt, taking over the responsibility of caring for us, and freeing us to be all he originally intended us to be. Add to this the fact that He is not only the Holy (a sanctuary, consecrated) One of Israel (his chosen people) but the God of the whole earth. My goodness! He is the highest authority in the universe....royalty of the highest degree....and we are his children.

We come into this life without much. Most of us do not know the life of royalty, so it is something we have to learn. Royalty is not a life of hanging out on a yacht, sunbathing, drinking champagne and eating bonbons. Oh sure, the younger royals can act like fools when they are growing into their royal place (most of us have had these times too), but they also learn pretty early that with that coveted standing in the world comes much more responsibility than the normal 'man on the street'.

The man on the street spends his time attempting to meet his own needs and often has little time to focus on greater things than how he can make what money he has stretch far enough this month. He doesn't know himself and so it isn't even an option to teach his children that they are children of royalty. Most of the time he is not aware of his responsibility in the overall scheme of life, therefore cannot pass knowledge he doesn't own to his young ones.

It is different, this royal responsibility. Their day to day needs are met. They are protected by bodyguards. When they find a humanitarian project they want to do, they don't worry about where the money is coming from....they just get crackin'....and things fall into place. Sure there could be some fund raisers, but they know many people of status and financial standing that will help support the right project. They have confidence, an expectation that their projects will succeed.

They have 'men from the street' taking care of much of the stuff that most of us would love to hand off to others....things like laying out their clothes (everything from laundry/dry-cleaning, ironing and putting away), bringing in the meals and afternoon tea, someone to drive them from place to place.

Having all of these activities taken care of opens them up to be able to take care of weightier responsibilities, the care of other people. Love is more often a born, maintained and grown through a sense of responsibility than butterfly feelings.

They balance this responsibility with enjoyment. Recreation with family, friends and business associates is as important for them as any blue collar worker. True royal behavior is humble, not haughty.

We have been let down by members of the human race. For some this happens once in a while, and for others it seems to happen more often than not. Trusting this unseen God who calls us royalty....who is promising things that resonate in our hearts, but contradicts what we see and what we have been taught....is a difficult transition that all do not make.

The reason for our Biblical studies is that when we reach out for more understanding, we are actually telling God of our desire for closeness. As with any relationship trust is built block by block, one fruitful experience after another.

Our learning is not only about the promises. We learn about the things that are God's responsibilities and which are ours. We learn how to deal with other people, how to act in integrity and what to do when we do not. We learn through the word and experience the depth of God's love for us and in turn we find that our capacity to love has been expanded.

I can't tell you how many times I have attempted to do things that are God's responsibility. I meant well, but stepped in when it didn't look like anything was happening. The unfortunate part about not having patience to see Him work in these situations was my actions in the circumstance often created a longer wait and sometimes had to be undone before His outcome could be seen.

For some reason we believe that God is only there for the 'big' things, but we learn that even those small things left to him work better. He is logical, precise and detailed. Our focus should be on him and his greatness, allowing him to work out the details of the dream. He does not give us a dream and then ask us to fill in all the blanks or make it come to pass in our own strength.

Good morning, Father. Thank you for your word that tells us that as we draw nigh to you, you draw nigh to us. As we understand more about your wishes for us, we can see the love behind your words and actions. Thank you for helping us to conduct our relationships in the earth in a similar fashion....by clearly communicating with others so that they understand our desire is for their good, for their health, prosperity and peace. Thank you for favor that so blankets us that it is felt by those we come in contact with....that it is seen by the masses. Show us that person you want us to touch today in a special way. In Jesus' name, we praise and thank you....Amen!

Definitions for today's study:

Maker - a primitive root; **to do or make**, in the broadest sense and widest application (as follows) :- accomplish, **advance**, appoint, apt, be at, become, bear, bestow, bring forth, bruise, be busy, × certainly, **have the charge of**, **commit**, deal (with), deck, + displease, do, (ready) dress (-ed), (put in) execute (-ion), exercise, fashion, + feast, [fight-] ing man, + finish, fit, fly, follow, fulfil, furnish, gather, get, go about, **govern**, grant, great, + hinder, hold ([a feast]), × indeed, + be industrious, + journey, keep, labour, maintain, make, be meet, observe, **be occupied**, offer, + officer, pare, bring (come) to pass, perform, practise, prepare, procure, **provide**, put, requite, × sacrifice, serve, set, shew, × sin, spend, × surely, take, × throughly, trim, × very, + vex, be [warr-] ior, work (-man), yield, **use**.

Husband - a primitive root; **to be master**; hence (as denominative from <H1167> (ba`al)) **to marry** :- **have dominion (over)**, be husband, marry (-ried, × wife); from <H1166> (ba`al); a master; hence a husband, or (figurative) owner (often used with another noun in modifications of this latter sense) :- + archer, + babbler, + bird, captain, chief man, + confederate, + have to do, + dreamer, those to whom it is due, + furious, those that are given to it, great, + hairy, he that hath it, have, + horseman, husband, lord, man, + married, master, person, + sworn, they of.

Lord - from <H1961> (hayah); (the) **self-Existent or Eternal**; **Jehovah, Jewish national name of God** :- Jehovah, the Lord. Compare <H3050> (Yahh), <H3069> (Yehovih).

Hosts - or (feminine) tseba'ah, tseb-aw-aw'; from <H6633> (tsaba'); **a mass of persons (or figurative things)**, especially reg. **organized for war (an army)**; by implication a campaign, literal or figurative (specifically hardship, worship) :- appointed time, (+) army, (+) battle, company, host, service, soldiers, waiting upon, war (-fare); a primitive root; **to mass (an army or servants)** :- assemble, fight, perform, muster, wait upon, war.

Name - primitive word [perhaps rather from <H7760> (suwm) **through the idea of definite and conspicuous position**;

compare <H8064> (shamayim)]; an appellation, **as a mark or memorial of individuality**; **by implication honor, authority, character** :- + base, [in-] fame [-ous], name (-d), renown, report **Redeemer** - a primitive root, **to redeem (according to the Oriental law of kinship)**, i.e. **to be the next of kin (and as such to buy back a relative's property, marry his widow, etc.)** :- × in any wise, × at all, **avenger**, deliver, (do, perform the part of near, next) kinsfolk (-man), **purchase**, **ransom**, redeem (-er), **revenger**.

Holy one - or qadosh, kaw-doshe'; from <H6942> (qadash); **sacred (ceremonial or moral)**; (as noun) **God (by eminence)**, an angel, a saint, **a sanctuary** :- holy (One), saint; a primitive root; to be (causat. make, pronounce or observe as) **clean** (ceremonial or moral) :- appoint, bid, **consecrate**, dedicate, defile, hallow, (be, keep) holy (-er, place), keep, prepare, proclaim, purify, sanctify (-ied one, self), × wholly.

Israel - from <H8280> (sarah) and <H410> ('el); **he will rule as God**; Jisraël, a symbolical name of Jacob; also (typically) of his posterity :- Israel; from <H8280> (sarah) and <H410> ('el); he will rule as God; Jisraël, a symbolical name of Jacob; **also (typically) of his posterity** :- Isreal + shortened from <H352> ('ayil); strength; as adjective mighty; especially the Almighty (but used also of any deity) :- God (god), × goodly, × great, idol, might (-y one), power, strong. Compare names in "-el."

God - plural of <H433> ('elowahh); gods in the ordinary sense; but **specifically used (in the plural thus, especially with the article) of the supreme God**; occasionally applied by way of deference to magistrates; and sometimes as a superlative :- angels, × exceeding, God (gods) (-dess, -ly), × (very) great, judges, × mighty; rarely (shortened) 'eloahh, el-o'-ah; probably prolonged (emphatic) from <H410> ('el); a deity or the Deity :- God, god. See <H430> ('elohiym); shortened from <H352> ('ayil); strength; as adjective mighty; especially the Almighty (but used also of any deity) :- God (god), × goodly, × great, idol, might (-y one), power, strong. Compare names in "-el."; from the same as <H193> ('uwl); probably strength; hence anything strong; specifically a chief (politically); also a ram (from his strength); a pilaster (as a strong support); an oak or other strong tree :- mighty (man), lintel, oak, post, ram, tree; from an unused root meaning to twist, i.e. (by implication) be strong; the body (as being rolled together); also powerful :- mighty, strength.

Whole earth - from an unused root probably meaning **to be firm**; **the earth** (at large, or partitively a land) :- × common, country, earth, field, ground, land, × nations, way, + wilderness, world.

Called - a primitive root [rather identical with <H7122> (qara') **through the idea of accosting a person met**]; to call out to (i.e. **properly address by name**, but used in a wide variety of applications) :- bewray [self], that are bidden, call (for, forth, self, upon), cry (unto), (be) famous, guest, invite, mention, (give) name, preach, (make) proclaim (-ation), pronounce, publish, read, renowned, say; a primitive root; to encounter, whether accidentally or in a hostile manner :- befall, (by) chance, (cause to) come (upon), fall out, happen, meet.

CHAPTER 8

Step up or Stand Down

Isaiah 54:6 (KJV)

6 For the LORD hath called thee (*you*) as a woman forsaken (*who has given up her power, position, or an advantage; especially when you did not want to*) and grieved (*carved, cut in pieces; in pain or anger; vexed, annoyed, confused, or worried*) in spirit (*that unseen part of you*), and a wife of youth (*the state of juvenility; the freshness and vitality characteristic of a young person, but also lacking and evidencing lack of experience of life*), when thou wast refused (*spurn, refuse with contempt someone's love or friendship*), saith thy God.

So many of the words written to us in the Bible speak of the abuses that take place between human beings. We spoke yesterday that our fight is not with the person who attacks us or the situation that seems to have been custom made to chip away at our confidence, but with the spirit behind the attack.

It is difficult for us to balance our responses in those times. Are we to step up and give a response or we are to just simply walk away from hurtful situations? Each time we face a new situation it is important to take our lead from God. There will be times he asks us to speak up, to make our side of the grievance known. There will be times when we will be asked to hold back, to allow him and him alone deal with the offender. Either way guidance from Him is necessary.

This verse speaks of the various threats to our heart peace. They are threats that we will be faced with in the future, that we have been faced with in the past. In some cases we have had to stand down in a situation and allow another to take a higher position or be in a position of advantage over us.

It is extremely difficult to allow someone else to take the lead position, especially when we feel it should be ours through experience or seniority. You may find that you are being asked to train that person or help them transition into that position you felt should be yours.

It hurts to have that other person in a position of power, but He will help you adjust your attitude and move forward. We feel vulnerable but show God through our obedience that we trust Him to care for us in this situation. This is an acknowledgment that He is truly in charge.

Keep in mind that these times are used by him to grow us, and undoubtedly the other person as well. He says here that he calls us in this position. He calls us when we feel as though we have been cut to pieces and are vexed. He calls us when we are rejected by people we want to be friends with, or those we love dearly.

Just as a good friend will call when they know you have been hurt, so does He. It is not a question of "if", but "when" these sad assaults will happen to our emotions. But there is something comforting in knowing that he meets with us in these situations.

He calls us by our name, and our name is sweet to him. He treats us like the royalty he so often reminds us we are. In His eyes, we are renowned, widely known and esteemed. This is the way he wants us to see ourselves. Sometimes we are overlooked in the process of getting to this elevated position.

These are the things of life he sees us through, provides for us in and redeems us out of. As any good parent will not allow their children's hurts go on forever, He loves us through.

During these times, we gain knowledge we will need in future phases of life. Along with this knowledge a deeper understanding of the whole picture and wisdom to walk confidently forward. We can gage if we helped to create the circumstance or not.

Understanding gives us tools to maneuver a future similar situation with ease. The skill to respond wisely is often gained only during troubling times. God's favor and grace bring us out on top.

Good morning, Father. Thank you for helping us to see that even the events in life that seem less than favorable for us, will be used in some beneficial twist in our lives. Your favor supersedes any difficulty we encounter….and even in those tight spots, the times it looks like we are being stepped on and over by another, when the advantage appears to go to the other person….we will with you come out on top. You comfort us through the heartache of rejection. Your love keeps us from sliding into bitterness that adversely flavors all relationships and work that we want to accomplish. You lift us up above any failure that bitterness would attempt to bring. Help us today to reach out to others who are hurting in any of these ways and lovingly call out their name so that they feel your presence. In Jesus' name, we praise and thank you....Amen!

Definitions for today's study:

Called - a primitive root [rather identical with <H7122> (qara') through **the idea of accosting a person met**]; **to call out to** (i.e. properly **address by name**, but used in a wide variety of applications) :- **bewray [reveal oneself]** [self], **that are bidden**, call (for, forth, self, upon), cry (unto), **(be) famous**, guest, invite, mention, (give) name, preach, (make) proclaim (-ation), pronounce, **publish**, read, **renowned [widely known and esteemed]**, say; a primitive root; to encounter, whether accidentally or in a hostile manner :- befall, (by) chance, (cause to) come (upon), fall out, happen, meet.

Woman - feminine of <H376> ('iysh) or <H582> ('enowsh); irregular plural nashiym, naw-sheem'; **a woman** (used in the same wide sense as <H582> ('enowsh)) :- [adulter]ess, each, every, female, × many, + none, one, + together, wife, woman. Often unexpressed in English; from <H605> ('anash); properly a mortal (and thus differing from the more dignified <H120> ('adam)); hence a man in general (singly or collectively) :- another, × [blood-] thirsty, certain, chap [-man], divers, fellow, × **in the flower of their age**, husband, **(certain, mortal) man**, people, person, servant, some (× of them), + stranger, those, + their trade. It is often unexpressed in the English Version, especially when used in apposition with another word. Compare <H376> ('iysh).

Forsaken - a primitive root; **to loosen**, i.e. **relinquish [to give up your power, position, or an advantage, especially when you do**

60

not want to do this], permit, etc. :- commit self, fail, **forsake [leave someone especially if they needed you]**, fortify, help, **leave (destitute, off)**, **refuse**, × surely.

Grieved - a primitive root; properly **to carve**, i.e. **fabricate or fashion**; hence (in a bad sense) **to worry, pain or anger** :- **displease**, grieve, **hurt**, make, be sorry, **vex**, worship, **wrest**.

Spirit - from <H7306> (ruwach); wind; by resemblance breath, i.e. a sensible (or even violent) exhalation; figurative life, anger, unsubstantiality; by extensive a region of the sky; by resemblance spirit, but only of a rational being (including its expression and functions) :- air, anger, blast, breath, × cool, courage, mind, × quarter, × side, spirit ([-ual]), tempest, × vain, ([whirl-]) wind (-y); a primitive root; properly to blow, i.e. breathe; only (literal) to smell or (by implication perceive (figurative to anticipate, enjoy)) :- accept, smell, × touch, make of quick understanding.

Wife – Same as 'woman' above

Youth - or na`ur, naw-oor'; and (feminine) ne`urah, neh-oo-raw'; properly passive participle from <H5288> (na`ar) as denominative**; (only in plural collective or emphatical) youth, the state (juvenility) or the persons (young people)** :- chlldhood, youth; from <H5287> (na`ar); (concrete) **a boy** (as active), from the age of infancy to adolescence; by implication **a servant**; also (by interchange of sex), a girl (of similar latitude in age) :- babe, boy, child, damsel [from the margin], lad, servant, young (man); a primitive root [probably identical with <H5286> (na`ar), **through the idea of the rustling of mane, which usually accompanies the lion's roar]**; to tumble about :- shake (off, out, self), overthrow, toss up and down; a primitive root; to growl :- yell.

Refused - a primitive root; **to spurn**; also (intransitive) to disappear :- abhor, cast away (off), contemn, despise, disdain, (become) loathe (-some), melt away, refuse, reject, reprobate, × utterly, vile person.

Saith - a primitive root; **to say** (used with great latitude) :- answer, appoint, **avouch**, bid, boast self, call, certify, challenge, charge, + (at the, give) command (-ment), commune, consider, declare, demand, × desire, determine, × expressly, × indeed, × intend, name, × plainly, promise, publish, report, require, say, speak (against, of), × still, × suppose, talk, tell, term, × that is, × think, use [speech], utter, × verily, × yet.

CHAPTER 9

In the Blink of an Eye

Isaiah 54:7 (KJV)

7 For a small (*cut off, short in duration, diminutive*) moment (*wink of the eyes*) have I forsaken (*relinquish give up power, position, or advantage...especially when you do not want to*) thee; but with great (*exceeding, mighty, large*) mercies (*sympathy for someone and doing something about it, great kindness toward the distressed*) will I gather (*to grasp, collect*) thee.

This verse was written before Jesus walked the earth. Isaiah 53 discussed His death, burial and resurrection. Isaiah 53:7 'Though mistreated, he was submissive - he did not open his mouth'. Isaiah 53:11 'After this ordeal, he will see satisfaction'.

The 53rd chapter speaks of a time when Jesus was cut off from God for a while as His purpose was being fulfilled. Jesus knew what was happening to him and why, as is evidenced by his prayer to the Father in the garden. And even though he understood his path and purpose, along with the satisfaction of the end result....there was a period toward the end when he said 'why have you forsaken me?'.

The first part of this chapter is for us to follow Jesus' lead. If he felt this way, it is inevitable we will at some point feel this way too. We too may feel cut off from God at times. For us especially early on in our relationship with him, our understanding is not as deep as Jesus' was. It is not uncommon for us to question the 'whys' of trials.

In the last chapter we talked about times we are hurt by people and circumstances of life. During these times we can feel as though God doesn't see our pain and/or that he doesn't care about what is happening. To use a phrase we hear a lot about in the media these days, these are all 'teaching' moments.

This verse speaks of a small moment, a diminutive wink of the eye or blink. One of the dictionary meanings of moment is 'an indefinitely short time'. This meaning may be how we see this promise played out, rather than an eye wink. We all remember times when it felt like we were hanging on by a thread for a long, long time.

But if this is like another mention of how God sees time (2 Peter 3:8), it could explain why it seems a lot longer than a mere blink. In the scope of eternity, a blink could mean a day(s), or week(s), or month(s) or year(s).

During this blink, we are required to build ourselves up, speak in faith that all will end well, reach out to others who need help (even if we feel like we need it more than they do) and sing our songs of triumph. During times when God seems to be blinking, we can begin a journey into our closest time with Him.

It happens because we tend to draw closer to him, ask him more questions about what has happened and what we are to do….and take more silent time to listen for direction from him when we are facing troubled times. It is our search for truth, and faith spoken during these times that motivates Him to 'with great mercies gather us in', not the circumstance or pain itself.

Good morning, Father. Thank you for greater understanding of your comprehension of time and the blink of an eye. These verses have given us so much to look forward to and we have yet to come into the bulk of promise that this chapter brings. We are so grateful for our lives….for understanding that we are here at this time and in this place for a special reason that is systematically being revealed to us….thank you for prayer that works and covers us and our families from the calamities of life. We pray for all those who have been affected by separation, death, sickness and/or loss of homes and belongings in any circumstance. Give us the resources to do what we as your children do best….pull together to help each other out in times of need. In Jesus' name, we praise and thank you….Amen!

Definitions for today's study:
Small - or qaton, kaw-tone'; from <H6962> (quwt); **abbreviated [cut short in duration]**, i.e. **diminutive**, literal (in quantity, size or number) or figurative (in age or importance) :- **least**, less (-ser), **little (one)**, small (-est, one, quantity, thing), young (-er, -est); a primitive root; properly **to cut off**, i.e. (figurative) detest :- be grieved, lothe self.
Moment - from <H7280> (raga`); **a wink (of the eyes)**, i.e. a very short space of time :- instant, moment, space, suddenly; a primitive root; properly to toss violently and suddenly (the sea with waves, the skin with boils); figurative (in a favorable manner) to settle, i.e. quiet; **specifically to wink (from the**

motion of the eye-lids) :- break, divide, find ease, be a moment, (cause, give, make to) rest, make suddenly.

Forsaken - a primitive root; **to loosen**, i.e. **relinquish [to give up your power, position, or an advantage, especially when you do not want to do this]**, permit, etc. :- commit self, fail, **forsake [leave someone especially if they needed you]**, fortify, help, **leave (destitute, off)**, **refuse**, × surely.

Great - or (shortened) gadol, gaw-dole'; from <H1431> (gadal); **great (in any sense)**; hence older; also insolent :- + aloud, elder (-est), + **exceeding (-ly)**, + far, (man of) great (man, matter, thing, -er, -ness), high, long, loud, **mighty**, more, much, noble, proud thing, × sore, (×) very; a primitive root; properly to twist [compare <H1434> (gedil)], i.e. **to be (causative make) large (in various senses, as in body, mind, estate or honor, also in pride)** :- advance, boast, bring up, exceed, excellent, be (-come, do, give, make, wax), great (-er, come to...estate, + things), grow (up), increase, lift up, magnify (-ifical), be much set by, nourish (up), pass, promote, proudly [spoken], tower; from <H1431> (gadal) (in the sense of twisting); thread, i.e. a tassel or festoon :- fringe, wreath.

Mercies - from <H7355> (racham**); compassion [a feeling of sympathy for someone who is in a bad situation because you understand and care about them, the humane quality of understanding the suffering of others and wanting to do something about it]** (in the plural); by extension the womb (as **cherishing the foetus**); by implication a maiden :- bowels, compassion, damsel, **tender love**, (great, tender) mercy, pity, womb; a primitive root; to fondle; by implication to love, especially to compassionate :- have compassion (on, upon), love, (find, have, obtain, shew) **mercy [showing great kindness toward the distressed]** (-iful, on, upon), (have) pity, Ruhamah, × surely.

Gather - a primitive root; **to grasp**, i.e. **collect** :- assemble (selves), **gather (bring) (together**, selves together, up), heap, resort, × surely, take up.

CHAPTER 10

Wrath? or Scratching the Surface?

Isaiah 54:8 (KJV)

8 In a little (*to mark out, as if scratched from the surface*) wrath (*a splinter, rage or strife*) I hid my face from thee for a moment (*wink of the eye*); but with everlasting (*eternal, past the vanishing point*) kindness (*favor, good deeds, loving-kindness*) will I have mercy (*fondle, touching lightly with affection with brushing movements; love, be compassionate to, have pity, mercy*) on thee, saith (*admit openly and bluntly, make no bones about it*) the LORD thy Redeemer.

Ok so let's get to it! No one likes to discuss the wrath of God. I don't! It tends to make me cringe....and especially when I first began to read through and study the Bible. Of course then my relationship was not so much like a friendship, or father-daughter scenario, but more like government official vs. a peon role in a tyrannical and abusive government.

I am not saying that this is how God saw it, but it was closer to my understanding of who God was at that time.

The first church I went to was torturous. I mean from the time you walked in the door for service until you got home and began your study again it was a tear-fest. I have to say I was born-again there, but I had been searching for something for a long time. I found the main thing there.

I believed that God had something better for me. However in this church rather than build people up with God's word, they would beat you down with it. The songs sung were about all the struggle and pain of following Him, continually walking in desert places.

The preaching took advantage of the fact that most of the folks going there didn't think they had much worth on the earth, let alone a place of worth in the kingdom. There wasn't a dry eye in the place. And during alter calls if you looked backward no one was left in the seats. The whole church got up to come forward to weep in remorse over sins of the past week.

Wrath was alive and well there. After a few long months, I left church. One Sunday continuing to cry on my way home I said 'God if this is the life in your kingdom you promised, I might as well go back to my old life!' I sure hadn't cried that much before coming to church. It felt like I had gone backwards instead of being better off for taking the step into the Kingdom.

Over the years I have come to understand that when I read the Bible and wrath is mentioned that I have a grace covering over me to protect me from wrath. The same goes for you. Jesus was sent here to reconcile a people whose face is turned from God back to him, we are those people. Through Jesus' work, we have been reconciled and covered with grace and favor.

If you look at the people he was close with way back when, you don't see displays of wrath in their lives either. Those in relationship were protected from wrath. It is God's desire to have a loving relationship with us that continues to draw us closer and closer. It doesn't mean we won't ever be corrected....we will. But that correction is not violent.

Just look at this word 'little', it means to scratch, we might see this as a thin wax covering on an apple. If you scratch that covering you will get small pieces of wax without touching the skin of the fruit. And 'wrath' here is a splinter, it is to crack off.

Even our closest relationships have moments (blink/wink of the eye periods of time) when you separate yourself from the other person. Sometimes this separation is momentary so that we will not be able to say or do something that will forever harm the other person and in turn the relationship. It is a protective move, so to speak. It is a move to protect the person from an act of anger, but also to protect ourselves.

God knows better than any human could know, the depths of pain brought on by angry outbursts. He knows the harm of an abusive relationship and he is not an abuser. He loves us so much that when he does feel this anger and turns his face from us for the blink of an eye, he can't stay away for longer than that.

As this says...with everlasting (past the vanishing point) favor, kindness, good deeds, love....he will touch us affectionately, like brushing our hair or sitting with his arm around us and brushing or patting our arm. That loving show of affection makes us want to snuggle into him, to nestle into our protected position with his grace covering us and favor providing for our every need.

And here it is again! He avouches for this. He is *admits this openly and bluntly; making no bones about it.* He would be an abusive person to redeem us from one harsh taskmaster only to become that in our lives. He can't be! It is not in him.

Good morning, Father. Thank you for helping us to look at this word 'wrath' through the veil of grace and favor brought to us through the work of Jesus. We understand that there are many things changing in the world that are less than favorable, but as your people you have promised us protection, love and victory. We ask for correction when we are heading in the wrong direction. We know that this correction is not what many tell us, it is not wrath and it is not harsh. Thank you for closing some doors and helping us to see this as one of your many methods of protection....thank you for the enjoyment of every minute. It is hard for us to get to any other step on the ladder of life without this joy....the joy of the Lord is our strength. We are obligated to bring joy wherever we go and to whomever we meet. We rebuke the worry about your wrath in order to walk fully in joy. You have said you will bless those who bless us and curse those who curse us....this applies to us as well. We look for someone to bless today and restrain ourselves from all cursing activity....no evil word or act against you or another. In Jesus' name, we praise and thank you....Amen!

Definitions for today's study:
Little - a primitive root; **to mark out**, i.e. (primitive) **scratch** or (defensive) imprint :- **scrabble**, set [a mark]

Wrath - from <H7107> (qatsaph); **a splinter** (as chipped off); figurative **rage or strife** :- foam, indignation, × **sore**, wrath; a primitive root; **to crack off**, i.e. (figurative) **burst out in rage** :- (be) anger (-ry), displease, fret self, (provoke to) **wrath** (come), be wroth.

Hid - a primitive root; **to hide** (by covering), literal or figurative :- be absent, keep close, **conceal**, hide (self), (keep) secret, × surely.

Face - plural (but always as singular) of an unused noun paneh, paw-neh'; from <H6437> (panah); **the face (as the part that turns)**; used in a great variety of applications (literal and figurative); also (with prepositional prefix) as a preposition (before, etc.) :- + accept, a- (be-) fore (-time), against, anger, × as (long as), at, + battle, + because (of), + beseech, **countenance**, edge, + employ, endure, + enquire, face, favour, fear of, for, forefront (-part), form (-er time, -ward), from, front, heaviness, × him (-self), + honourable, + impudent, + in, it, look [-eth] (-s), × me, + meet, × more than, mouth, of, off, (of) old (time), × on, open, + out of, over against, the partial, person, + please, presence, propect, was purposed, by reason, of, + regard, right forth, + serve, × shewbread, sight, state, straight, + street, × thee, × them (-selves), through (+ -out), till, time (-s) past, (un-) to (-ward), + upon, upside (+ down), with (-in, + - stand), × ye, × you; a primitive root; to turn; by implication to face, i.e. appear, look, etc. :- appear, at [even-] tide, behold, cast out, come on, × corner, dawning, empty, go away, lie, look, mark, pass away, prepare, regard, (have) respect (to), (re-) turn (aside, away, back, face, self), × right [early].

Moment - from <H7280> (raga`); **a wink (of the eyes)**, i.e. a very short space of time :- instant, moment, space, suddenly; a primitive root; properly to toss violently and suddenly (the sea with waves, the skin with boils); figurative (in a favorable manner) to settle, i.e. quiet; **specifically to wink (from the motion of the eye-lids)** :- break, divide, find ease, be a moment, (cause, give, make to) rest, make suddenly.

Everlasting - or olam, o-lawm'; from <H5956> (`alam); properly **concealed**, i.e. **the vanishing point**; generally **time out of mind** (past or future), i.e. (practical) eternity; frequent adverb (especially with prepositional prefix) always :- **alway (-s)**, ancient (time), any more, continuance, **eternal**, (for, [n-]) ever (-lasting, -more, of old), lasting, long (time), (of) old (time), perpetual, at any time, (beginning of the) world (+ without end). Compare <H5331> (netsach), <H5703> (`ad); a primitive root; to veil from sight, i.e. conceal (literal or figurative) :- × any ways, blind, dissembler, hide (self), secret (thing).

Kindness - from <H2616> (chacad); kindness; by implication (towards God) piety; rarely (by opposition) reproof, or (subjective) beauty :- **favour, good deed** (-liness, -ness), **kindly, (loving-) kindness, merciful** (kindness), mercy, pity, reproach, wicked thing; a primitive root; properly perhaps to bow (the neck only [compare <H2603> (chanan)] in courtesy to an equal), i.e. to be kind; also (by euphemism [compare <H1288> (barak)], but rarely) to reprove :- shew self merciful, put to shame

Mercy - a primitive root; **to fondle**; by implication **to love**, especially **to compassionate** :- have compassion (on, upon), love, (find, have, obtain, shew) mercy (-iful, on, upon), (have) pity, Ruhamah, × surely.

Saith - a primitive root; **to say** (used with great latitude) :- answer, appoint, **avouch [admit openly and bluntly; make no bones about]**, bid, boast self, call, **certify**, challenge, charge, + (at the, give) command (-ment), commune, consider, declare, **demand**, × **desire, determine**, × expressly, × indeed, × **intend**, name, × plainly, **promise**, publish, report, **require**, say, speak (against, of), × still, × suppose, talk, tell, term, × that is, × think, use [speech], utter, × verily, × yet

Redeemer - a primitive root, **to redeem (according to the Oriental law of kinship)**, i.e. **to be the next of kin (and as such to buy back a relative's property, marry his widow, etc.)** :- × in any wise, × at all, **avenger**, deliver, (do, perform the part of near, next) kinsfolk (-man), **purchase, ransom**, redeem (-er), **revenger**.

72

CHAPTER 11

Confirmations & Confederate Activity

Isaiah 54:9 (KJV)

9 For this is as the waters of Noah (*the patriarch of the flood, quiet, settled down, be confederated or someone who assists in a plot/plan*) unto me: for as I have sworn (*to be complete, to seven oneself, command solemnly, by an oath*) that the waters of Noah should no more go over (*cross over, any transition*) the earth; so have I sworn that I would not be wroth (*vehemently condemn, extremely angry at something unjust or wrong*) with thee, nor rebuke (*censure or severely or angrily criticize, corrupt, reprove or take to task*) thee.

Always a truth is expressed at least two and usually more typically multiple times in the Bible. This is done for verification to the reader. These multiple renderings of the same word or principle act as confirmation of a truth.

In the last chapter we were talking of God's wrath and that it is not in him to be an abusive father or taskmaster to us. Now today this verse is confirmation of that truth.

The story used as an example is the story of Noah and the flood. Now the flood was a perfect example of wrath. God vehemently condemned the <u>acts</u> of the people who had completely given themselves up to ungodly forces and lifestyle.

But, he is not in the habit of leaving those who are in relationship with him hanging in the lurch. He had a human partner who completed the daunting task of building an immense ship.

If we look at Noah's name we see a couple of interesting aspects of his character. The first is that he was quiet or settled. If he were not, he would have never been able to endure being the talk of the community for taking on this project. People had to think he had flipped his lid.

Secondly when God discussed the situation with Noah, he enlisted him as a confederate. He ended up being the one person in the earth that assisted God in the plan.

He was quiet, silently plodding ahead with this God made plan. He was quiet in spite of the fact that he was the one person who was following God amongst a sea of crazy acting folks.

Once the plan was completely carried out God swore that there would never be a time like this again when he destroyed by flood all but a sliver of civilization. (see Genesis 9:11) Side note: Hmmm....9:11? Destruction? No word meaning coincidence in Hebrew. I don't know what this means, but it is interesting.

If we look at the track record of this promise, there has never been another such flood. The flood as best as we can tell happened over 3,500 years ago. Looks to me like God has made good on this promise!

And if he made good on that, then would we be wrong in assuming we can depend on the promise that we will not experience him vehemently condemning us, or being extremely angry at any unjust or wrong act we have committed?

His promise to Noah has been proven true. So when he said he would not severely or angrily criticize us or take us to task, we can also take this to the bank. Now considering he has made this statement about his willingness to forget our past, is it really right for us to hold our own wrong doings against ourselves? Is it time to forgive ourselves for past wrongs that we have done? I think it is.

Good morning, Father. Thank you for this confirmation of your love without criticism, your correction without wrath. Remind us each time we fall into self-condemnation about your stand on this subject. If we believe this precept, then we are fighting with you spiritually if we continue to condemn that which you have chosen to love us through. Give us wisdom that when we hang onto self-condemnation we are setting up barriers against your glory manifesting in our relationships, in our business and community activities. Although it may seem 'right' to beat ourselves up and pay for a wrong we did....Jesus already paid for that (redeemed us from that) and according to your word doing this serves no good purpose. More importantly, by doing so we are discounting Jesus' work in our lives. If you don't hold these things against us, neither should we. Just as you enlisted Noah as a confederate to assist in and carry out your plan, so do we take up our individual confederate activity....walking out our purpose in the earth. Give us the opportunity to discuss this with others, so that they can begin to walk in the freedom this affords. Your favor is massive and envelopes our every activity today. In Jesus' name, we praise and thank you....Amen!

Definitions for today's study:
Waters - dual of a primitive noun (but used in a singular sense); **water**; figurative juice; by euphemism urine, semen :- + piss, wasting, **water (-ing, [-course, -flood, -spring])**.

Noah - the same as <H5118> (nuwach); rest; Noäch, **the patriarch of the flood** :- Noah; or nowach, no'-akh; from <H5117> (nuwach); **quiet** :- **rest (-ed, -ing place)**; a primitive root; to rest, i.e. **settle down**; used in a great variety of applications, literal and figurative, intransivitive, transitive and causative (to dwell, stay, let fall, place, let alone, withdraw, give comfort, etc.) :- cease, **be confederate [someone who assists in a plot]**, lay, let down, (be) quiet, remain, (cause to, be at, give, have, make to) rest, set down. Compare <H3241> (Yaniym).

Sworn - a primitive root; properly **to be complete**, but used only as a denominative from <H7651> (sheba`); **to seven oneself**, i.e. **swear (as if by repeating a declaration seven times)** :- **adjure [command solemnly, ask or request earnestly]**, **charge (by an oath, with an oath)**, feed to the full [by mistake for <H7646> (saba`)], take an oath, × straitly, (cause to, make to) swear; or (masculine) shib`ah, shib-aw'; from <H7650> (shaba`); a primitive cardinal number; seven (as the sacred full one); also (adverb) seven times; by implication a week; by extension an indefinite number :- (+ by) seven ([-fold], -s, [-teen, -teenth], -th, times). Compare <H7658> (shib`anah).

Go over - a primitive root; **to cross over**; **used very widely of any transition** (literal or figurative; transitive, intransitive, intensive or causative); specifically to cover (in copulation) :- alienate, alter, × at all, beyond, bring (over, through), carry over, (over-) come (on, over), conduct (over), convey over, current, deliver, do away, enter, escape, fail, gender, get over, (make) go

76

(away, beyond, by, forth, his way, in, on, over, through), have away (more), lay, meddle, overrun, make partition, (cause to, give, make to, over) pass (-age, along, away, beyond, by, -enger, on, out, over, through), (cause to, make) + proclaim (-amation), perish, provoke to anger, put away, rage, + raiser of taxes, remove, send over, set apart, + shave, cause to (make) sound, × speedily, × sweet smelling, take (away), (make to) transgress (-or), translate, turn away, [way-] faring man, be wrath.

Earth - from an unused root probably meaning **to be firm**; **the earth** (at large, or partitively a land) :- × common, country, earth, field, ground, land, × nations, way, + wilderness, world.

Wroth - a primitive root; **to crack off**, i.e. (figurative) **burst out in rage** :- (be) anger (-ry), displease, fret self, (provoke to) wrath (come), **be wroth [vehemently incensed and condemnatory].**

Rebuke - a primitive root; **to chide [censure severely or angrily]**:- **corrupt [to encourage someone to start doing dishonest, illegal, or immoral things]**, **rebuke [to tell someone that they have behaved badly. The usual word is tell off]**, **reprove [take to task]**.

CHAPTER 12

Covenants, More Durable than Mountains

Isaiah 54:10 (KJV)

10 For the mountains (*mountain range or hills, to loom up*) shall depart (*the idea of receding by contact, withdraw*), and the hills be removed (*to waver, to slip, be fallen in decay*); but my kindness (*beauty, favor, good deeds, loving kindness, merciful*) shall not depart from thee, neither shall the covenant (*in the sense of cutting, a compact-because made by passing between pieces of flesh*) of my peace (*completeness, wholeness, health, wealth, happiness*) be removed, saith (*admit openly and bluntly, make no bones about it*) the LORD that hath mercy (*to lovingly brush, hold, love, be compassionate*) on thee.

At first glance this looks like it means that the mountains and hills <u>will definitely</u> depart and be removed....but, the way the Hebrew seems to be written states this a little differently. This sounds a little more like 'even if the mountains were to recede and the hills were to fall away in decay....' God is using a scenario that would be highly unlikely to happen.

The definition for depart in the dictionary means 'move away from a place into another direction'. This scenario would have the mountain picking up its skirt and moving away from its present location, like relocating from Denver to Illinois.

The Strong's Concordance definition is through the idea of receding by contact. This scenario would be like erosion which does take hundreds of centuries to accomplish....The Rockies may look different than they did in the beginning through contact with rain and wind and human progress, but they are still there.

He stands this up in comparison against the likelihood of his promised actions and heart attitude toward us being removed or eroding over time. He wants us to consider just how unlikely it is that he would walk away from his covenant with us, or just losing interest in us like a fickle lover.

He is the one that initiated the covenant. He is obligated by his own oath to us to stand by and complete his part of the covenants he has entered into. We know that there are times when we don't measure up to our side of the bargain.

Our loving God has made provision that sustains us even during these times through the work that his son Jesus performed. That work has placed us in a state of justification, a state of righteousness. This is a gift we could never repay.

That covenant guarantees us that he will never leave, or fail, or forsake us. This covenant is full of favor, good deeds, loving-kindness, beauty, and mercy. The 'shalom' or overall well-being (which includes, safety/protection, happiness, welfare, health, heart peace, prosperity, favor, recompense for things that have been taken or lost, repayment, amends)....this word covers it all.

It is the whole enchilada as far as the good life is concerned. And again, he is decreeing 'I am openly and bluntly admitting this is yours from me....make no bones about it, this is for you to claim as your own.' He has mercy on us, holding us in his arms. It is as if while sitting in his lap, he is brushing our hair and giving us that little squeeze of encouragement....he paves the way before us.

Good morning, Father. Thank you for giving us a comparison that your kindness, favor, and shalom cannot be taken from us any more than a mountain range could vanish into thin air. Let's face it mountains are solid and have been standing for centuries upon centuries....but you Lord are so much more solid than this hard and fast creation of yours. As you have mentioned to us in other writings, the created thing cannot be greater than the creator....so our natural conclusion is that you stand by your word. As humans we have been let down by others who have promised love or certain behaviors....and our prayer is that when we feel any element of doubt crop up about the stability of your feelings toward us, that you alert us to that lie and helps us to lift you up. As a by-product of lifting you up, we too will be built up in our faith. As your favor flows and overflows in our lives we thank you in advance for showing us who we can share our surplus with. In Jesus' name, we praise and thank you....Amen!

Definitions for today's study:
Mountains - a shorter form of <H2042> (harar); **a mountain or range of hills** (sometimes used figurative) :- hill (country),

81

mount (-ain), × promotion; from an unused root meaning **to loom up**; a mountain :- hill, mount (-ain).

Depart - a primitive root [perhaps rather the same as <H4184> (muwsh) **through the idea of receding by contact**]; to **withdraw** (both literal and figurative, whether intrans. or trans.) :- cease, depart, go back, remove, take away; a primitive root; to touch :- feel, handle.

Hills - feminine from the same as <H1387> (Geba`); **a hillock** :- hill, little hill; from the same as <H1375> (gebiya`); a hillock; Geba, a place in Palestine :- Gaba, Geba, Gibeah; from an unused root (meaning to be convex); a goblet; by analogy the calyx of a flower :- house, cup, pot.

Removed - a primitive root; **to waver**; by implication **to slip**, shake, fall :- be carried, cast, be out of course, **be fallen in decay**, × exceedingly, fall (-ing down), be (re-) moved, be ready, shake, slide, slip.

Kindness - from <H2616> (chacad); kindness; by implication (towards God) piety; rarely (by opposition) reproof, or (subjective) beauty :- **favour**, **good deed** (-liness, -ness), **kindly**, **(loving-) kindness**, **merciful** (kindness), mercy, pity, reproach, wicked thing; a primitive root; properly perhaps to bow (the neck only [compare <H2603> (chanan)] in courtesy to an equal), i.e. to be kind; also (by euphemism [compare <H1288> (barak)], but rarely) to reprove :- shew self merciful, put to shame

Covenant - from <H1262> (barah) (**in the sense of cutting** [like <H1254> (bara')]); **a compact (because made by passing between pieces of flesh)** :- confederacy, [con-]feder[-ate], covenant, league; a primitive root; to select; also (as denominative from <H1250> (bar)) to feed; also (as equivalent. to <H1305> (barar) to render clear (Eccl. 3:18) :- choose, (cause to) eat, manifest, (give) meat;

Peace - or shalom, shaw-lome'; from <H7999> (shalam); **safe**, i.e. (figurative) **well**, **happy**, friendly; also (abstract) **welfare**, i.e. **health**, **prosperity**, **peace** :- × do, familiar, × fare, **favour**, + friend, × great, (good) health, (× perfect, such as be at) peace (-able, -ably), prosper (-ity, -ous), rest, **safe (-ty)**, salute, welfare,

(× all is, be) well, × wholly; a primitive root; to be safe (in mind, body or estate); figurative to be (causative make) completed; by implication to be friendly; by extension to reciprocate (in various applications) :- **make amends**, (make an) end, finish, full, give again, make good, **(re-) pay (again)**, (make) (to) (be at) peace (-able), that is perfect, perform, (make) prosper (-ous), **recompense**, render, requite, make restitution, restore, reward, × surely.

Saith - a primitive root; **to say** (used with great latitude) :- answer, appoint, **avouch [admit openly and bluntly; make no bones about]**, bid, boast self, call, **certify**, challenge, charge, + (at the, give) command (-ment), commune, consider, declare, **demand**, × **desire**, **determine**, × expressly, × indeed, × **intend**, name, × plainly, **promise**, publish, report, **require**, say, speak (against, of), × still, × suppose, talk, tell, term, × that is, × think, use [speech], utter, × verily, × yet

Mercy - a primitive root; **to fondle**; by implication **to love**, especially **to compassionate** :- have compassion (on, upon), love, (find, have, obtain, shew) mercy (-iful, on, upon), (have) pity, Ruhamah, × surely

CHAPTER 13

Transition, Utilitarian to Lavish

Isaiah 54:11 (KJV)

11 O thou afflicted (*depressed in mind or circumstances, needy, poor; being looked down on or browbeaten*), tossed (*throw carelessly*) with tempest (*a violent commotion or disturbance*), and not comforted (*to sigh, be consoled, avenged, ease*), behold (*see with attention*), I will lay (*imbed*) thy stones (*to build; carbuncle which is a garnet without facets, highly reflective*) with fair (*light or pale*) colours, and lay thy foundations (*establish*) with sapphires (*a gem, to score with a mark as a tally or record*).

The Complete Jewish Bible shows this verse as 'Storm-ravaged [city], unconsoled, I will set your stones in the finest way, lay your foundations with sapphires.'

The word afflicted covers a lot of ground, ground that each of us unfortunately has traveled during the course of our time on earth. At one point or another we all have been depressed emotionally or in our circumstances (i.e. a financial depression). There are times when we find ourselves in need.

At other times we have been the brunt of someone looking down on us or browbeating us in order to get the upper hand over us in a situation. Here he is talking to us.

This verse and the next reference precious gems stones, let's see how they fit in. Precious gems are used many times in the Bible. Although I don't know an in-depth analogy or meaning of each gem, we have a very base understanding that these precious gems are valuable. Gemstones also reflect light rather than being dense like another type of stone or a brick or concrete block.

They generally have a greater financial worth than colored pieces of glass, or a stone that has a coat of paint slapped on it. In this verse the reference is to building our foundations with stones (or carbuncles, basically a garnet without facets) and sapphires. This is just not the normal earthly foundation.

Foundations are usually built with brick, or stone (certainly not gemstones), or concrete….durable, but not necessarily beautiful. Foundations in a normal construction project are utilitarian not lavish.

God doesn't think that way. In his eyes we are his royal children. I'm all for the mansions that are promised to us in the sweet by and by….however, in more than one place of the Bible He states his desire for us to have not just utilitarian provision in life, but also the lavish. He replaces the drab and every day with that which is beautiful.

As a matter of fact, if you consider his descriptions of heaven they are to us lavish. He is accustomed to this….he is accustomed to the best. I am not so sure he even looks at the idea of building a foundation with concrete.

It is something that would get the job done but doesn't cost as much as gemstones would. We think of these things, but he owns everything. Would he be concerned with the cost? I'm not so sure he thinks of this as lavish, but instead normal.

Could it be that if we took him at his word (here and elsewhere) and were to look at this as the norm that we would not always be striving for this part of his will being done, but instead expecting he will do it for us? I mean this verse says that 'HE will lay thy stones....and lay thy foundations'. It doesn't say that WE will lay or make an effortful attempt to attain this goal (strive).

Is it our small thinking that hinders us from having bigger and better? Is it our misguided understanding of His word, that makes us choose to shoulder this responsibility rather than leaving it to Him?

If we are in his image and we are to emulate him (his thoughts, his words, and his deeds) then perhaps we should be meditating on his thought processes where this is concerned. He wants our lives painted with light and festive colors that will reflect the good and beautiful to the world.

Good morning, Father. Thank you for scratching the surface of a truth here that we have not fully grasped....I know I do not fully understand, but am asking for each of us to have both understanding and then the wisdom to walk in it. Thank you for taking us from whatever sad or depressed state we may find ourselves in to a place where we can absorb and reflect your light. Each of us have a different understanding of what a beautifully decorated life will look like, it is part of the diversity that you love so much. Whatever vision you have planted as seed in each of us comes closer to manifesting in our lives each time we take time to close our eyes and imagine you building it for us stone by precious gemstone. Help us to see that what we call extravagant, lavish, audacious….you call normal. These are your words and we need to embrace them just as we do the principle of helping others or receiving healing. Help us to see that with your 'normal' we are able to influence and help others far more than what our idea of lavish ever could. Prepare our minds and hearts for stepping into your specific vision for us. In Jesus' name, we praise and thank you….Amen!

Definitions for today's study:
Afflicted - from <H6031> (`anah); **depressed, in mind or circumstances** [practically the same as <H6035> (`anav), although the margin constantly disputes this, making <H6035> (`anav) subjective and <H6041> (`aniy) objective] :- **afflicted**, humble, lowly, **needy, poor**; a primitive root [possibly rather identical with <H6030> (`anah) **through the idea of looking down or browbeating**]; to depress literal or figurative, transitive or intransitive (in various applications, as follow) :- abase self, afflict (-ion, self), answer [by mistake for <H6030> (`anah)], chasten self, deal hardly with, **defile**, exercise, force, gentleness, humble (self), hurt, ravish, sing [by mistake for <H6030> (`anah)], speak [by mistake for <H6030> (`anah)], submit self, weaken, × in any wise; or [by intermixture with <H6041> (`aniy)] anayv, aw-nawv'; from <H6031> (`anah); depressed (figurative), in mind (gentle) or circumstances (needy, especially saintly) :- humble, lowly, meek, poor. Compare <H6041> (`aniy).
Tempest - a primitive root; **to rush upon**; by implication to toss (transitive or intransitive, literal or figurative) :- be (toss with) **tempest [a violent commotion or disturbance]**(-uous), **be sore**

troubled, come out as a (drive with the, **scatter with a) whirlwind**.

Comforted - a primitive root; prop. **to sigh**, i.e**. breathe strongly**; by implication to be sorry, i.e. (in a favorable sense) to pity, **console** or (reflex.) rue; or (unfavorably) **to avenge (oneself)** :- comfort (self), **ease** [one's self], repent (-er, -ing, self).

Lay - a primitive root; **to crouch (on all four legs folded, like a recumbent animal)**; by implication **to recline**, repose, brood, lurk, **imbed** :- crouch (down), fall down, make a fold, lay, (cause to, make to) lie (down), make to rest, sit.

Stones - from the root of <H1129> (banah) **through the meaning to build**; a **stone** :- + **carbuncle [a garnet without facets]**, + mason, + plummet, [chalk-, hail-, head-, sling-] stone (-ny), (divers) weight (-s); a primitive root; to build (literal and figurative) :- (begin to) build (-er), **obtain children, make, repair**, set (up), × surely.

Fair colors - from an unused root **meaning to paint**; **dye (specifically stibium for the eyes)** :- fair [light or pale] colours, **glistering**, paint [-ed] (-ing).

Foundations - a primitive root; **to set** (literal or figurative); intensive **to found**; reflexive to **sit down together**, i.e. settle, consult :- appoint, take counsel, **establish, (lay the, lay for a) found (-ation)**, instruct, lay, ordain, set, × sure.

Sapphires - from <H5608> (caphar); **a gem** (perhaps as used for scratching other substances), **probably the sapphire** :- sapphire; a primitive root; properly **to score with a mark as a tally or record**, i.e. (by implication) **to inscribe**, and also **to enumerate [to name each one of a series or list of things, determine the number or amount of]**; intensitive to recount, i.e. celebrate :- commune, (ac-) count, **declare**, number, + penknife, reckon, scribe, shew forth, speak, talk, tell (out), writer.

CHAPTER 14

Pressure Points - What's the Hurry?

Isaiah 54:12 (KJV)

12 And I will make thy windows of agates (*rubies*) , and thy gates of carbuncles (*a fiery stone, crystals or diamond*), and all thy borders of pleasant (*valuable things, favor, pleasure, desire*) stones (*to build, stone, a mason*).

In the last chapter we began discussing the idea of God making our living quarters. Earlier studies have taught us that we are not to worry about a roof over our heads, food and drink to nourish us, or clothing to cover and decorate our bodies. Those studies taught us that when we first seek his kingdom and his righteousness, when this direction is followed all these things will be added to us.

In both verses, he states that he will lay our foundations, make our windows and gates and all of our borders. He states it is his job not ours. His promise is that all of these are made of the finest of materials.

We also looked at the fact that this will be a little different for each person. God's love of diversity of personalities, textures, colors and materials is evident throughout creation.

For some people a log cabin is their thing of beauty, finely hewn logs….polished and lined up perfectly and sealed. The interior will be furnished with natural woods and comfortable cushions….but, will carry through on the natural outdoor'sy theme. God prefers this over a shack in the woods with a dirt floor and sparse hard furnishings.

For some people this will be a Victorian, 15,000 square foot mansion. Again there will be a plethora of ornate furnishings also made of natural materials but with a more refined slant. God prefers this over a one bedroom apartment in the projects.

From one end of the spectrum of pictures God places in our hearts to the other….he is the one who has promised this picture to reveal itself in our natural/physical/material life. He said he will build it and give it to us. And he states this outward show will be a reflection that will draw others to him through us.

There has been a certain something that has been on my mind about this idea of _striving_ to do and to be in God's purpose. The idea of finding that purpose brings pressure that often pushes people into decisions that move them away from the vision rather than toward it.

Take care not to be led off track by paying attention to the promise that 'these ten steps will accelerate your progress', instead of being patient during a time of seasoning. Is it not better to wait for that God appointed person or deal to be revealed by Him?....rather than striving and stressing yourself out? Striving = Stress. Waiting patiently = heart peace.

God knows our hearts, he knows our shortcomings and what character adjustments are needed. Those areas corrected will allow us to handle expanded influence with people, elevated standing within our communities, ultimate success in our business lives, and the material show of that financial success with grace. God will not place in our hand something we are not prepared for and could destroy us until we have matured.

Could it be that we have made a bit more of this idea of living in your purpose and doing everything we can to find that purpose and then press, press, press? Has this undo added pressure to lives that are already filled with pressure from outside influences created a striving oriented society, rather than a people who are more interested in being settled in and resting in God's plan?

The deeper I have gotten into these studies the more I see God has laid upon himself many of the tasks of getting things done that we incorrectly think we need to make happen ourselves. James 1:22 teaches that we have to be not hearers only, but doers of the word. We need to take this more seriously.

Not in the way many teach. Instead it would be wise to see exactly what our current task is and doing that. At the same time we need to understand more clearly God's responsibility as he has clearly stated. Then let him do it and get out of his way.

I am not saying that we should not plan or work. I am not saying we don't have something to do while waiting for

God's stated provision (and it is more than just enough to get us through today). The thought that continues to recur in my mind is, the essence of a statement made in The Last Samurai. *I think a man does what he can, until his destiny is revealed. ~Nathan Algren.* There is wisdom in this statement.

Just as this character found his purpose while he was recovering from battle wounds, overcoming alcoholism brought on by past despicable acts in his life, and being a 'prisoner', so do we come to ourselves (and God) during times when we are doing nothing of great import rather than striving for a goal. During this time he sought spiritual fulfillment, kept a journal, closed his eyes and focused (meditated) on his past and present.

Our part is seeking understanding of what righteous standing means, learning what He has promised in our relationship, and doing whatever task is there for us to do each day. Then exercise patience, allowing him to bring to us the people and yes, even the material things he has promised.

We might agree that there are many people who do not live to their potential or who live what seems a mediocre life. Is that for us to judge? We don't see the big picture. A person who looks lazy or non-committed could be in a time of centering and seasoning before God places in their hands the outward material blessings promised.

It would be wise to step away from noisy detractors. Instead we could work at becoming the person he wants us to be, and understand the value of expecting he will deliver what he has promised. We can know that we do not have to strive, but instead rest in righteousness waiting patiently for them to manifest.

Good morning, Father. Thank you for your word and for patience when a few words don't seem to be enough. I pray for each of these and their deepening relationship with you. In Jesus' name, we praise and thank you....Amen!

Definitions for today's study:

Make - or siym, seem; a primitive root; **to put** (used in a great variety of applications, literal, figurative, inference and elliptis) :- × any wise, appoint, bring, call [a name], care, cast in, change, charge, commit, consider, convey, determine, + disguise, dispose, do, get, give, **heap up**, hold, impute, lay (down, up), leave, look, make (out), mark, + name, × on, ordain, order, + paint, place, preserve, purpose, put (on), + regard, rehearse, reward, (cause to) set (on, up), shew, + stedfastly, take, × tell, + tread down, ([over-]) turn, × wholly, work.

Windows - from an unused root meaning **to be brilliant**; the sun; by implication **the east**; figurative a ray, i.e. (architectural) **a notched battlement** : + east side (-ward), sun ([rising]), + west (-ward), window. See also <H1053> **(Beyth Shemesh)= beth-house + shemesh-of the sun**

Agates - from the same as <H3537> (kad) in the **sense of striking fire from a metal forged; a sparkling gem**, probably **the ruby** :- agate; from an unused root meaning **to deepen**; properly a pail; but generically of earthenware; a jar for domestic purposes :- barrel, pitcher.

Gates - from <H8176> (sha`ar) in its original sense; **an opening**, i.e. **door or gate** :- **city**, door, gate, port (× -er; a primitive root; to split or open, i.e. (literal, but only as denominative from <H8179> (sha`ar)) to act as gate-keeper (see <H7778> (show`er)); (figurative) to estimate :- think.

Carbuncles - from <H6916> (qiddah); burning, i.e. a carbuncle or **other fiery gem** :- carbuncle; from <H6915> (qadad); cassia bark (as in shrivelled rolls) :- cassia; a primitive root; to shrivel up, i.e. contract or bend the body (or neck) in deference :- bow (down) (the) head, stoop.

Borders - or (shortened) gebul, gheb-ool'; from <H1379> (gabal); properly **a cord (as twisted)**, i.e. (by implication) **a boundary**; by extension the territory inclosed :- border, bound, coast, × great, **landmark**, limit, quarter, space; a primitive root; properly to twist as a rope; only (as a denominative from <H1366> (gebuwl)) to bound (as by a line) :- **be border**, set (bounds about).

Pleasant - from <H2654> (chaphets); **pleasure; hence (abstract) desire**; concrete **a valuable thing**; hence (by extension) a matter (as something in mind) :- **acceptable**, delight (-some), desire, things desired, matter, pleasant (-ure), purpose, willingly; a primitive root; properly to incline to; by implication (literal but rarely) to bend; figurative **to be pleased with**, desire :- × any at all, (have, take) delight, desire, **favour**, like, move, be (well) pleased, have pleasure, will, would.

Stones - from the root of <H1129> (banah) through the meaning **to build**; **a stone** :- + carbuncle, + **mason**, + plummet, [chalk-, hail-, head-, sling-] stone (-ny), (divers) weight (-s); a primitive root; to build (literal and figurative) :- (begin to) build (-er), obtain children, make, repair, set (up), × surely.

CHAPTER 15

Whispered Layers of Understanding

Isaiah 54:13 (KJV)

13 And all thy children (*builder of family name, house, relationship, quality or condition*) shall be taught (*instructed, disciple, learned, properly to goad-a verbalization that encourages you to attempt something*) of the LORD; and great (*abundant in quantity, size, age, number, rank and quality*) shall be the peace (*safety, well, happy, friendly, welfare, health, prosperity, favor, recompense, restoration*) of thy children.

This verse brings us more information on our children (figuratively ideas or brain children). If you remember verse:1 spoke about barren people having a promise of more children than those who are married.

In the strictest literal terms children means a son, the builder of the family name or a house. Figuratively children can mean relationships, subjects (under authority and control of a government or country)....it can mean quality or condition....or being very fruitful....or to build.

If we focus on the children aspect we can see that this is a verse of great comfort to parents. To the barren among us who may not have their own children but instead have nieces and nephews, children from the church or neighborhood with whom you are close. It could mean your following – men and women who have come to you for greater understanding in some subject (this could be your business, or from a group you lead at church or in the community, or even your social media).

The promise is that these children whether natural or 'adopted' are taught of the Lord. This word 'of' is translated a couple different ways and I believe each fits. Of can mean both 'about' and 'from/by'.

So it can look like 'will be taught about the Lord', or it can look like 'will be taught from/by the Lord'. The Bible is the book of life. It is the book about Jehovah God and in essence is our owner's manual. By following the precepts he lays out for us, the 'good life' emerges.

As either figurative or literal parents we are the conduit by which our children learn about God and these guidelines for living. Even when we don't use His name within the context of some teaching moment, if the precepts match his guidelines, they are being taught of the Lord.

Our greatest understanding comes not by the words of the teacher or text we are reading or the circumstance experienced. But it comes through God whispering layers upon layers of understanding to us while the teacher, text or circumstance is before us.

And so it is for those we teach. Information comes to us and our children/students (whether the written word or through an experience or through an encounter with a teacher) and the understanding of the information and the wisdom to use it properly is inspired by God. Even as we pass along our knowledge to others, the inspiration to understand comes from our Father.

Our teaching others encourages them to attempt things they may have had in their heart for some time. Without encouragement the dream could remain hidden for years. The process of sharing our experiences and knowledge helps others gain the courage needed to move forward on their dream. And once they do....

Once the student has achieved a level of success in his own right, it becomes their time to teach. It is interesting to note that teachers rarely stop being students. There are always new topics or deeper levels of knowledge in our field to learn. The learning cycle never stops.

The result of passing teachings onto our children (students/clients/co-workers) is that both the student and the teacher begin to walk in greater and greater peace. I don't believe that a teacher can really say they know a subject until they have first experiential knowledge and then taken the time to pass the information on to someone else.

Something wonderful happens when truth is laid out in an orderly form. The teaching of truth and orderly processes dispels confusion and along with it strife. With these two aggravators of peace removed, peace is ushered in.

At one time I looked at peace as our dictionary definition describes 'the absence of mental stress or anxiety'. But as we have come through our study here, we see that it means this and so much more in the Hebrew. We need to continually remember that this word, shalom or what has been translated peace, is watered down by our English understanding.

Please take the time to read through the definition below and look at our other studies on this subject. You will begin to see how profound this really is. One of the biggest part of studying we do here is to go beyond our English thought process and begin to see more clearly expanded understanding of these words.

Good morning, Father. Thank you for our own shalom and the shalom we have been enabled to bring to others through teaching moments. Thank you for encouraging us through understanding more and more detail. We choose today to live a life that is not lackadaisical....but instead full of follow through to serve others. We know that we won't accomplish anything if we fail to step out. Help us to see through your instructive word the difference between your responsibility and ours, that timing is all important in any successful plan, and that even those things that may feel like a delay have been placed there for a reason. You will point out our next step, if we will ask and then wait for the answer. We choose today to take our next step only when we feel a heart peace about this move. Keep us from manipulation in any form because we know that manipulation brings pressure that can cause us to make wrong decisions for our lives. Thank you for the understanding that our decisions do not only affect us, but have a ripple effect throughout our circle of family, friends and associates. Thank you for understanding this mantle of responsibility that you have given us as parents and teachers brings with it responsibility. We will be held accountable for our decisions and what we choose to teach or withhold....this is not meant as a condemnation but instead as a head's up to always and with your guidance do our best. Give us supernatural understanding to help others in our walk today. In Jesus' name, we praise and thank you....Amen!

Definitions for words from today's study:

Children - from <H1129> (banah); <u>a son (as a builder of the family name)</u>, in the widest sense (of literal and figurative <u>relationship</u>, including grandson, <u>subject</u>, <u>nation</u>, <u>quality or condition</u>, etc., [like <H1> ('ab), <H251> ('ach), etc.]) :- + afflicted, age, [Ahoh-] [Ammon-] [Hachmon-] [Lev-]ite, [anoint-]ed one, appointed to, (+) arrow, [Assyr-] [Babylon-] [Egypt-] [Grec-]ian, one born, bough, branch, breed, + (young) bullock, + (young) calf, × came up in, child, colt, × common, × corn, daughter, × of first, + firstborn, foal, + **very fruitful**, + postage, × in, + kid, + lamb, (+) man, meet, + mighty, + nephew, old, (+) people, + rebel, + robber, × servant born, × soldier, son, + spark, + steward, + stranger, × surely, them of, + tumultuous one, + valiant[-est], whelp, **worthy**, young (one), youth; a primitive root; to build (literal and figurative) :- (begin to) build (-er), **obtain children**, make, **repair**, set (up), × surely.

Taught - or limmud, lim-mood'; from <H3925> (lamad); **instructed** :- **accustomed**, **disciple**, **learned**, taught, **used**; a primitive root; **properly to goad [a verbalization that encourages you to attempt something]**, i.e. (by implication) **to teach** (the rod being an Oriental incentive) :- [un-] accustomed, × diligently, expert, instruct, learn, skilful, teach (-er, -ing).

Great - by contracted from <H7231> (rabab); **abundant (in quantity, size, age, number, rank, quality)** :- (in) abound (-undance, -ant, -antly), captain, **elder**, **enough**, **exceedingly**, **full**, great (-ly, man, one), **increase**, long (enough, [time]), (do, have) many (-ifold, things, a time), ([ship-]) master, **mighty**, **more**, (too, very) much, multiply (-tude), officer, often [-times], **plenteous**, populous, prince, **process [of time]**, suffice (-ient); a primitive root; properly to cast together [compare <H7241> (rabiyb)], i.e. increase, especially in number; also (as denominative from <H7233> (rebabah)) to **multiply by the myriad** :- increase, be many (-ifold), be more, multiply, **ten thousands**

Peace - or shalom, shaw-lome'; from <H7999> (shalam); **safe**, i.e. (figurative) **well**, **happy**, friendly; also (abstract) **welfare**, i.e. **health**, **prosperity**, **peace** :- × do, familiar, × fare, **favour**, + friend, × great, (good) health, (× perfect, such as be at) peace (-able, -ably), prosper (-ity, -ous), rest, **safe (-ty)**, salute, welfare, (× all is, be) well, × wholly; a primitive root; to be safe (in mind, body or estate); figurative to be (causative make) completed; by implication to be friendly; by extension to reciprocate (in various applications) :- **make amends**, (make an) end, finish, full, give again, make good, **(re-) pay (again)**, (make) (to) (be at) peace (-able), that is perfect, perform, (make) prosper (-ous), **recompense**, render, requite, make restitution, restore, reward, × surely.

CHAPTER 16

Oppression & Terror Eliminated

Isaiah 54:14 (KJV)

14 In righteousness (*uprightness as a consequence of being honorable and honest, justice-fair and morally right or result*) shalt thou be established (*fixed, prepared, applied to*): thou shalt be far from oppression (*injury, defrauding, distress, cruelty, extortion, being pressed on, violated, having violence against*); for thou shalt not fear (*dread, afraid, in reverence of*): and from terror (*dissolution of, destruction, dismay, ruin, being laid hold of*); for it shall not come near (*approach, be at hand, present, produced, stand, take*) thee.

In Isaiah 53, Jesus' work was foretold. His redeeming work completed or established our righteous stand with God. We receive this righteous stance, by first coming to a realization that we need this relationship then confess this need.

In Matthew 6, we studied about all things being added to us when we first seek his kingdom and his righteousness. It is paramount to our forward movement to understand more and more the full extent of this righteousness, and exactly what it means for us to have this standing. This and other chapters state the truth of our righteous standing, but if we do not accept that in our hearts and minds, it will be difficult to see the full benefit of this prevail in our lives.

Righteousness is not a feeling; it is a fact. We need to 'catch' ourselves when we move away from a righteous thought process to that of a sin based thought process.

Believing that we have been made righteous helps us to act righteously, not the other way around. And when we do something that offends other people or God, we need to remind ourselves that this one act alone does not wipe out that righteous stand.

Even with the best intent, we as humans mess up. We succumb to pressure and let's face it, sometimes we choose to do wrong things even though we know better. I am not saying that there is never any consequence to wrong doing, but I also believe strongly in the grace provided to us through Jesus' work.

He tells us here that we are fixed in this promised righteous stand. When we ask Jesus to come in and make us and our life what it was intended to be, a part of that process is asking forgiveness of sin. 1 John 1:9 tells us when we do '…he is faithful and just to forgive us our sins, and to cleanse us from all unrighteousness'.

This cleansing is not a temporary thing. It is a cleansing that first takes place in our spirit. It takes some time for the soul and body to catch up. This righteousness begins to change our mind, will, emotions and body to fall in line with righteous outward acts. This righteousness is like a veil so that when God sees us, he sees the perfection of

Jesus instead of the imperfections of the human standing before him.

Our righteous stand places us in yet another unique position, far from oppression because in righteousness (being conscious of our righteousness) there is no fear. Whenever we fall prey to fear or dread, it opens the door to oppression in all its forms. These include injury, defrauding, distress, cruelty, extortion, violated, or having violence acted out against us. But even terror, destruction, dismay, ruin and being laid hold of won't show up.

Why? Because when you know that you are the righteousness of God in Christ Jesus and you understand the love that is behind this relationship and what has been done for you....fear cannot get a foothold in your life. Fear might come knocking on your door, but you don't have to let it in.

Your study and meditation will make you strong enough in mind and heart to turn away from fear and stand firmly in the righteousness Jesus bought and paid for with his life. As a result of your study, you will more clearly understand the truths that rule God's kingdom and his righteousness. It will become clear what his responsibilities are and what responsibilities are yours.

Good morning, Father. Thank you for the cleansing that was made available for us through Jesus' work on the cross, for helping us to realize that forgiveness is a done deal. We have been forgiven of wrongs in the past, present and future. If that work were not complete, Jesus would have to drop back by often and redo this work, but as he said, "It is finished". Thank you for this written word that we can speak out loud. My prayer is for all who have followed this study that they will make this whole chapter part of their confessions. Each verse has held wonderful promise on its own, but as a whole chapter it paints a picture of success, protection, strength and prosperity. When confessed it becomes part of our spirit person, as this happens, believing and knowing occur. Manifestation follows suit. Thank you that righteousness eliminates fear. Oppression has been separated from us, and terror cannot stand in front of us because of this righteous stand. Thank you that our minds and hearts are strong in this righteous understanding. Through this strength we are able to serve so many more than we could before. In Jesus' name, we praise and thank you for it....Amen!

Definitions for today's study:

Righteousness - from <H6663> (tsadaq); **rightness** (abstract), subjective (**rectitude, uprightness as a consequence of being honorable and honest**), objective (justice), moral (virtue) or figurative (**prosperity**) :- justice, moderately, right (-eous) (act, -ly, -ness); a primitive root; to be (causative **make) right** (in a moral or forensic sense) :- cleanse, clear self, (be, do) just (-ice, -ify, -ify self), (be, turn to) righteous (-ness).

Established - a primitive root; properly **to be erect** (i.e. stand perpendicular); hence (causative) **to set up**, in a great variety of applications, whether literal (**establish, fix, prepare, apply**), or figurative (**appoint, render sure, proper or prosperous**) :- certain (-ty), confirm, direct, faithfulness, fashion, fasten, firm, be fitted, be fixed, frame, be meet, ordain, order, perfect, (make) preparation, prepare (self), provide, make provision, (be, make) ready, right, set (aright, fast, forth), be stable, (e-)stablish, stand, tarry, × very deed.

Far - a primitive root; **to widen (in any direction)**, i.e. (intransitive) recede or (transitive) remove (literal or figurative, of place or relation) :- (a-, be, cast, drive, get, go, keep [self], put, remove, be too, [wander], withdraw) far (away, off), loose, × refrain, very, (be) a good way (off).

Oppression - from <H6231> (`ashaq); **injury**, **fraud**, (subjective) **distress**, (concrete) **unjust gain** :- **cruelly**, **extortion**, oppression, thing [deceitfully gotten]; a primitive root (compare <H6229> (`asaq)); **to press upon**, i.e. oppress, defraud, **violate**, overflow :- get deceitfully, deceive, defraud, drink up, (use) oppress ([-ion], -or), **do violence** (wrong).

Fear - a primitive root; **to fear**; moral **to revere**; causative **to frighten** :- affright, be (make) afraid, **dread** (-ful), (put in) fear (-ful, -fully, -ing), (be had in) reverence (-end), × see, terrible (act, -ness, thing).

Terror - from <H2846> (chathah); properly a dissolution; concrete a ruin, or (abstract) consternation :- **destruction**, **dismaying**, **ruin**, terror; a primitive root; to **lay hold of**; especially to pick up fire :- heap, take (away).

Near - a primitive root; **to approach** (causative bring near) for whatever purpose :- (cause to) approach, (cause to) bring (forth, near), (cause to) come (near, nigh), (cause to) draw near (nigh), go (near), **be at hand**, join, be near, offer, **present**, **produce**, make ready, **stand**, **take**.

CHAPTER 17

Your Mission, if You Choose to Accept It

Isaiah 54:15 (KJV)

15 Behold, they shall surely gather together, but not by me: whosoever shall gather together against thee shall fall for thy sake.

Complete Jewish Bible - Any alliance that forms against you will not be my doing; whoever tries to form such an alliance will fall because of you.

New International Version - If anyone does attack you, it will not be my doing; whoever attacks you will surrender to you.

New Living Translation - If any nation comes to fight you, it is not because I sent them. Whoever attacks you will go down in defeat.

Young's Literal Translation - Lo, he doth diligently assemble without My desire, Who hath assembled near thee? By thee he falleth!

The Message - If anyone attacks you, don't for a moment suppose that I sent them, And if any should attack, nothing will come of it.

I like looking at different versions of the Bible. It helps to solidify my understanding of the words. This clearly states that the harsh alliances or attacks against us in life are not instigated by God. "Don't for a moment suppose I sent them". "lo, he doth assemble without my desire". "it is not because I sent them". "it will not be my doing. It sounds pretty clear to me.

But our programming over the years may have sounded quite different. Many times we cry out when in a tough spot. We hear people who don't know much about God and how this kingdom operates saying that this or that situation is 'an act of God'.

We may have said 'God never gives us any problem that we can't handle.' These statements are in direct conflict with Isaiah 54:15 and other supporting statements in this guide book. God promises good things for his people. James 1:17 "Every good and perfect gift is from above…"

The Bible also states that there will be forces or the people who are used by these forces coming against us in one way or another. It could come in the form of a slight that might hurt our feelings or on the other end of the spectrum a wrenching betrayal. These things can have little lasting effect on us if we tap into the righteousness available in our relationship.

Although this is true we will still have varying emotional, physical and mental responses to the attacks. It is a simple direction to say 'No' to attacks as they occur, or to the way we might want to respond. But I will admit that it is not always easy, especially in the beginning.

In the midst of attack it will take focus and diligence to hold onto and lean on what we know about God. That is why it is so necessary for us to retrain our minds and to hone our ability to catch ourselves when our minds begin to stray from our understanding about our righteous stand with God.

Fear will attempt to torment us into feeling that we should bow down to the attacks or attackers. This fear will come knocking on your door. Believing God has you covered and that nothing can come of it if you place your trust in His process will be your mission/assignment if you choose to accept it.

Good morning, Father. Thank you for the love you have for us, a love that wraps us up and keeps us safe. We also know that our affiliation with you doesn't mean that we will never be attacked. Like every other Christ follower, as your disciples we will encounter problems in life. Our difference from the world is the peace and victory that comes in our relationship. Some walk into this relationship with the faith of a child right from the start; others are logic based and have to be convinced through prayer and study. You love us all, no matter where we are in our path. We thank you for opportunities today to reach out and help someone else in their life today. In Jesus' name, we praise and thank you....Amen!

Definitions used in today's study:
Gather together - a primitive root; properly **to turn aside from the road (for a lodging or any other purpose)**, i.e. sojourn (as a guest); also to shrink, **fear (as in a strange place)**; also **to gather for hostility** (as afraid) :- abide, **assemble**, be afraid, dwell, fear,

gather (together), inhabitant, remain, sojourn, stand in awe, (be) stranger, × surely.

Not - from <H656> ('aphec); cessation, i.e. an end (especially of the earth); often used adverbially no further; also (like <H6466> (pa`al)) the ankle (in the dual), as being the extremity of the leg or foot :- ankle, but (only), end, howbeit, **less than nothing**, nevertheless (where), **no**, **none** (beside), **not** (any, - withstanding), thing of nought, save (-ing), there, uttermost part, want, without (cause); a primitive root; to disappear, i.e. cease :- be clean gone (at an end, brought to nought), fail.

Whosoever - an interrogative pronoun of persons, as <H4100> (mah) is of things, who (occasionally, by a peculiar idiom, of things); also (indefinite) whoever; often used in oblique construction with prefix or suffix :- any (man), × he, × him, + O that! what, which, **who (-m, -se, -soever)**, + would to God; or mah, mah; or ma, maw; or ma, mah; also meh, meh; a primitive particle; properly interrogative what (including how why when); but also exclamation what! (including how!), or indefinite what (including whatever, and even relative that which); often used with prefixes in various adverb or conjunction senses :- how (long, oft, [-soever]), [no-] thing, what (end, good, purpose, thing), whereby (-fore, -in, -to, -with), (for) why.

Fall - a primitive root; to fall, in a great variety of applications (intransitive or causative, literal or figurative) :- be accepted, cast (down, self, [lots], out), cease, die, divide (by lot), (let) **fail**, (cause to, let, make, ready to) fall (away, down, -en, -ing), fell (-ing), fugitive, have [inheritance], inferior, **be judged** [by mistake for <H6419> (palai)], lay (along), (cause to) lie down, light (down), be (× hast) lost, lying, **overthrow**, **overwhelm**, **perish**, present (-ed, -ing), **(make to) rot**, slay, **smite out**, × surely, **throw down**.

CHAPTER 18

Corruption & Interconnecting Timeframes

Isaiah 54:16 (KJV)

16 Behold, I have created the smith that bloweth the coals in the fire, and that bringeth forth an instrument for his work; and I have created the waster to destroy.

Complete Jewish Bible - It is I who created the craftsman who blows on the coals and forges weapons suited to their purpose; I also created the destroyer to work havoc.

The Message - I create the blacksmith who fires up his fore and make a weapon designed to kill. I also create the destroyer

The interesting thing here to me is that we are all in one sense or another, smiths. We create things. We develop our skills and material instruments. We do this for our work.

The word "work" as used here is described as an action, either good or bad. We have choices each day, each circumstance we encounter, to use these instruments for good or bad. It is our choice.

We have some fine instruments in today's world. Social media, the internet it runs on, riding lawn-mowers, Kitchen-Aids, the computer, smart phones, cars, trains and planes; and a myriad of other instruments that have been originally intended for good and helpful uses.

We have been given the ability to create with our minds, speech and physical actions. We have the responsibility to use all of these good gifts well. These tools, or words, or instruments can be turned into weapons by ill meaning people.

When we look at "the waster to destroy", we see it could have as easily been written "the corruptor who corrupts". There is still much I don't entirely understand about how God thinks. However, from my experience, more is revealed to me as I need the information. I cannot answer the question of 'why would a loving God create evil or a destroyer', for now it seems above my pay grade. I just know it is so.

I suppose it could be that we grow best when there is some resistance. If life were utopia, we would never know how good things are when they are good. Stop and think about it, would we know what good is if there were not bad in our lives. If all things in life were good, our choices would not carry as much weight. There would be no potential downside to be concerned with.

We have the choice to live our lives with not only good intent, but follow through. And when we do, things are better, a lot better. Perfection does not happen until we are on the other side. Even when we treat folks well, they can and sometimes will turn around and betray us or walk away.

It all is part of the big picture. Our life lessons never end. We move in and out of the interconnecting timeframes of life, with each of our decisions toward either good or bad culminating in the picture of our life to that point in time.

If we have been making a lot of bad decisions (using instruments in the wrong way) we have the opportunity to change the story of our lives through new and better decisions (better use of the instruments available to us).

In yesterday's study we were told evil or corrupt use of instruments will happen, but it doesn't come from God. But what happens when it is an outside force that is creating havoc against us? Tomorrow's study will answer that question for us.

Good morning, Father. Thank you for faith to see and believe even when we don't fully understand. Thank you for the motivation to move toward increasingly higher places of good in our lives and that when we slip and slide toward using the instruments you have provided for us in a wrong way that you are there to help us make the right decision. And even when we mess up you don't just cast us out, your guidance brings us back. Thank you for love is greater than our shortcomings and that Jesus' work has granted us grace for these times. Show us today the people you would like us to help. In Jesus' name, we praise and thank you....Amen!

Definitions for today's study:
Created - a primitive root; (absolute) **to create**; (qualified) to cut down (a wood), **select**, feed (as formative processes) :- choose, create (creator), cut down, dispatch, do, **make** (fat).

Smith - from <H2790> (charash); **a fabricator of any material** :- **artificer**, (+) carpenter, **craftsman**, engraver, **maker**, + mason, skilful, (+) smith, worker, **workman**, such as wrought.

Bloweth - a primitive root; **to puff**, in various applications (literal, to inflate, blow hard, scatter, **kindle**, expire; figurative, to disesteem) :- blow, breath, give up, cause to lose [life], seething, snuff.

Coals - perhaps from an unused root probably meaning **to be black**; **a coal**, whether charred or live :- coals.

Fire - a primitive word; **fire** (literal or figurative) :- **burning**, fiery, fire, flaming, hot.

Bring forth - a primitive root; to go (causattively bring) out, in a great variety of applications, literal and figurative, direct and proximate :- × after, **appear**, × assuredly, bear out, × begotten, **break out**, **bring forth** (out, up), carry out, come (abroad, out, thereat, without), + be condemned, depart (-ing, -ure), draw forth, in the end, escape, exact, fail, fall (out), fetch forth (out), get away (forth, hence, out), (able to, cause to, let) go abroad (forth, on, out), going out, grow, have forth (out), issue out, lay (lie) out, lead out, pluck out, proceed, pull out, put away, be risen, × scarce, send with commandment, shoot forth, spread, spring out, stand out, × still, × surely, take forth (out), at any time, × to [and fro], utter.

Instrument - from <H3615> (kalah); **something prepared**, i.e. **any apparatus** (as an implement, utensil, dress, vessel or weapon) :- armour ([-bearer]), artillery, bag, carriage, + furnish, furniture, instrument, jewel, that is made of, × one from another, that which pertaineth, pot, + psaltery, sack, stuff, thing, tool, vessel, ware, weapon, + whatsoever; a primitive root; to end, whether intransitive (to cease, be finished, perish) or transitive (to complete, prepare, consume) :- accomplish, cease, consume (away), determine, destroy (utterly), be (when...were) done, (be an) end (of), expire, (cause to) fail, faint, finish, fulfil, × fully, × have, leave (off), long, bring to pass, wholly reap, make clean riddance, spend, quite take away, waste.

Work - from <H6213> (`asah); **an action (good or bad)**; generally **a transaction**; abstract activity; by implication a product (specifically a poem) or (generic) property :- act, art, + bakemeat, business, deed, do (-ing), labour, thing made, ware of making, occupation, thing offered, **operation**, possession, × well, ([handy-, needle-, net-]) work, (-ing, -manship), wrought; a primitive root; to do or make, in the broadest sense and widest application (as follows) :- accomplish, advance, appoint, apt, be at, become, bear, bestow, bring forth, bruise, be busy, × certainly, have the charge of, commit, deal (with), deck, + displease, do, (ready) dress (-ed), (put in) execute (-ion), exercise, fashion, + feast, [fight-] ing man, + finish, fit, fly, follow, fulfil, furnish, gather, get, go about, govern, grant, great, + hinder, hold ([a feast]), × indeed, + be industrious, + journey, keep, labour, maintain, make, be meet, observe, be occupied, offer, + officer, pare, bring (come) to pass, perform, practise, prepare, procure, provide, put, requite, × sacrifice, serve, set, shew, × sin, spend, × surely, take, × throughly, trim, × very, + vex, be [warr-] ior, work (-man), yield, use.

Waster - a primitive root; **to decay**, i.e. (causative) **ruin** (literal or figurative) :- **batter**, cast off, **corrupt** (-er, thing), **destroy (-er**, -uction), **lose**, mar, **perish**, spill, **spoiler**, × utterly, waste (-r).

Destroy - a primitive root; **to wind tightly** (as a rope), i.e. **to bind; specifically by a pledge**; figurative **to pervert**, destroy; also to **writhe in pain** (especially of parturition) :- × at all, band, bring forth, (deal) **corrupt** (-ly), destroy, **offend**, lay to (take a) pledge, **spoil**, **travail**, × very, withhold.

CHAPTER 19

Trouble Brewing?

Isaiah 54:17 (KJV)

17 No weapon (*whatsoever, tool*) that is formed against thee shall prosper (*become mighty, push forward or advance*); and every tongue (*babbler, evil speaker, language, accusation, slander*) that shall rise (*succeed*) against thee in judgment (*a verdict, a sentence or formal decree, penalty, adversary*) thou shalt condemn (*declare wrong, disturb, violate, make trouble for, do wickedly*). This is the heritage (*occupancy, an estate, possession, distribution*) of the servants (*worshipper, bond-service*) of the LORD, and their righteousness (*right standing, justification, prosperous, cleansed*) is of me, saith (*whispered prophesy*) the LORD.

We ended the last chapter with this question. *'But what happens when it is an outside force that is creating havoc against us?'* Any tool, whatsoever is formed against us will not become mighty and nothing that anyone says against will succeed in doing damage.

A great promise for sure. From early in my life as a disciple of Jesus, this verse helped me through many days. As with many people out there, my life before I came into this family had its share of personal and financial drama.

This particular verse brought me great comfort during times of attack by old habits, thoughts and invitations to slide back into acting the way I used to. I was just beginning to stand on God's promises in hard times and this verse is one that helped me through.

I venture a guess that many politicians and other people in the public eye need to lean on this often. There is no shortage of people in the world who will attempt to devise a plan or fashion words meant to hurt you. Stop and think of the number of times that the media will take a sentence out of context to make an opponent look bad. It happens all the time.

This is also a cloaked caution to us about our own plans and words that we may have regarding another person. If we knew out of the gate the repercussion of us speaking badly about another person, or realized the trouble we brew for ourselves when we speak or do harm toward another, it would makes us think twice before we execute our plan.

It occurs to me that some of the most cherished and well-remembered people in history were people who would not speak negatively about other people. Some of these were people who no doubt had diametrically opposed stands in policy or religious leanings. Yet they were able to make inroads through disciplining their thoughts, tongue and actions, inroads that another may not have made.

Now I am not saying they never had feelings or thoughts that made them want to act in an undisciplined manner. But when the thought came, they chose to discipline themselves, short-stopping any negative action or words.

In this particular case, we are the subject of an attack. Gratefully the promise is that these attacks will not succeed. However, God is saying that it will happen because there are no shortages of naysayers.

There will be times when we will have to stand up and declare that the attack is wrong and at other times we will be asked to remain silent and depend on God as our defender.

I used to experience this in morning meetings at an old position. This was a roundtable scenario. All department heads were there and all major issues of daily operation were discussed in this meeting. In the beginning, I was not invited to the meetings because I was not at senior staff level.

For several months, a couple of times a week, the plant manager and another manager or two would come to my desk in an accusatory fashion after these meetings. The common complaint was that either replacement parts or supplies had run out, and the accusation was that they either hadn't been order or were delayed.

I would research the situation, and sometimes spend hours gathering backup documentation to my point of view and stand in the subject. Seldom did the results of my research prove the accusations correct.

After one of these accusations, I asked the plant manager if I could begin to attend the meetings. His response was less that warm, basically telling me that if I'd like to attend I could. So I said that unless he wanted me there and felt that it would be of some benefit to all there that I would choose not to attend.

Several days later, one of the staff came to me and said that I was being asked by the plant manager to attend these morning meetings. With me there, I was able to take notes on projects coming up or in process and ask questions that showed my concern for the smooth operation of the plant.

It also allowed me to offer the benefit of my experience in several areas in regard to the commodities I had worked with and familiar. When someone would say that something hadn't been done by my department, I'd be able to either refute the statement or give reason (i.e. not having the proper documentation to move forward).

Being privy to problems as they arose we were able to decide if it was necessary for us to expedite services or supplies to accommodate temporary expanded usages. The by-product of standing up and offering a "fix" to the problem of false accusations against my department was more harmony. There were very few times, if any, when these accusing delegations would come to my desk.

With more open lines of communication, the team leaders and managers would involve me at the front of the problem rather than at the end. Their confidence in my input to resolve issues was expanded, and we operated as a team rather than as adversaries.

Standing against false accusation, whether in the physical/material sense or on the battlefield in our mind, is a part of our estate with the Lord. When we choose to occupy our righteous stand, we disturb the attacks that come to us.

Good morning, Father. Thank you for helping us through those times when we are "thrown under the bus", for giving us the strategies to foil or disturb these attacks, and knowing in our hearts that success is ultimately ours. Attacks against us sometimes feel as though they are gaining traction, but ultimately any accusation or slander does not succeed. Give us open eyes to discern the truth of these matters, and help us examine ourselves. If there is any truth in the complaint shape our character so that we own this and apologize when necessary. There is nothing more destructive to our integrity than not owning our mistakes and making amends when necessary. Thank you for our righteous stand in your kingdom, and for showing us where we can best help someone else today. In Jesus' name, we praise and thank you....Amen!

Definitions for today's study:
Weapon - from <H3615> (kalah); **something prepared**, i.e. **any apparatus** (as an implement, utensil, dress, vessel or weapon) :- **armour** ([-bearer]), artillery, bag, carriage, + furnish, furniture, instrument, jewel, that is made of, × one from another, that which pertaineth, pot, + psaltery, sack, stuff, thing, **tool**, vessel, ware, weapon, + **whatsoever**; a primitive root; to end, whether intransitive (to cease, be finished, perish) or transitive (to complete, prepare, consume) :- accomplish, cease, consume (away), determine, destroy (utterly), be (when...were) done, (be an) end (of), expire, (cause to) fail, faint, finish, fulfil, × fully, × have, leave (off), long, bring to pass, wholly reap, make clean riddance, spend, quite take away, waste.
Formed - probably identical with <H3334> (yatsar) (through the **squeezing into shape**); ([compare <H3331> (yatsa`)]); **to mould** into a form; especially as a potter; figurative to determine (i.e. form a resolution) :- × earthen, fashion, form, frame, make (-r), potter, purpose; a primitive root; to press (intrans.), i.e. be narrow; figurative be in distress :- be distressed, be narrow, be straitened (in straits), be vexed.

Prosper - or tsaleach, tsaw-lay'-akh; a primitive root; to push forward, in various senses (literal or figurative, transitive or intransitive) :- break out, come (mightily), go over, be good, be meet, be profitable, (cause to, effect, make to, send) prosper (-ity, -ous, -ously).

Prosper - or tsaleach, tsaw-lay'-akh; a primitive root; **to push forward**, in various senses (literal or figurative, transitive or intransitive) :- break out, **come (mightily)**, go over, be good, be meet, be profitable, (cause to, effect, make to, send) prosper (-ity, -ous, -ously).

Tongue - or lashon, law-shone'; also (in plural) feminine leshonah, lesh-o-naw'; from <H3960> (lashan); **the tongue** (of man or animals), used literal (as the instrument of licking, eating, or speech), and figurative (**speech**, an ingot, a fork of flame, a cove of water) :- + **babbler**, bay, + **evil speaker**, **language**, talker, tongue, wedge; a primitive root; properly to lick; but used only as a denominative from <H3956> (lashown); to wag the tongue, i.e. to calumniate :- **accuse**, **slander**.

Rise - a primitive root; to rise (in various applications, literal, figurative, intensive and causative) :- abide, accomplish, × be clearer, confirm, continue, decree, × be dim, endure, × enemy, enjoin, get up, make good, help, hold, (help to) lift up (again), make, × but newly, ordain, **perform**, pitch, raise (up), rear (up), remain, (a-) **rise (up)** (again, against), rouse up, set (up), (e-) stablish, (make to) stand (up), stir up, strengthen, **succeed**, (as-, make) sure (-ly), (be) up (-hold, -rising).

Judgment - from <H8199> (shaphat); properly **a verdict** (favorable or unfavorable) pronounced judicially, especially **a sentence or formal decree** (human or [participle] divine law, individual or collective), including the act, the place, the suit, the crime, and **the penalty**; abstract justice, including a participle right, or privilege (statutory or customary), or even a style :- + **adversary**, ceremony, charge, × crime, custom, desert, **determination**, discretion, disposing, due, fashion, form, to be judged, judgment, just (-ice, -ly), (manner of) law (-ful), manner, measure, (due) order, ordinance, right, sentence, usest, ×

worth, + wrong; a primitive root; to judge, i.e. pronounce sentence (for or against); by implication to vindicate or punish; by extension to govern; passive to litigate (literal or figurative) :- + avenge, × that **condemn**, contend, defend, execute (judgment), (be a) judge (-ment), × needs, plead, reason, rule.

Condemn - a primitive root; to be (causative do or **declare) wrong**; by implication to **disturb**, **violate** :- condemn, **make trouble**, vex, be (commit, deal, depart, **do) wicked (-ly**, -ness).

Heritage - from <H5157> (nachal) (in its usual sense); prop. **something inherited**, i.e. (abstract) **occupancy**, or (concrete) an heirloom; generally **an estate**, patrimony or portion :- heritage, to inherit, inheritance, **possession**. Compare <H5158> (nachal); a primitive root; to inherit (as a [figurative] mode of descent), or (generally) to occupy; causative to bequeath, or (generally) **distribute**, instate :- divide, have ([inheritance]), take as an heritage, (cause to, give to, make to) inherit, (distribute for, divide [for, for an, by], give for, have, leave for, take [for]) inheritance, (have in, cause to, be made to) possess (-ion).

Servants - from <H5647> (`abad); a servant :- × bondage, bondman, [bond-] servant, (man-) servant; a primitive root; to work (in any sense); by implication to serve, till, (causative) enslave, etc. :- × be, keep in bondage, be bondmen, **bond-service**, compel, do, dress, ear, execute, + husbandman, keep, labour (-ing man), bring to pass, (cause to, make to) serve (-ing, self), (be, become) servant (-s), do (use) service, till (-er), transgress [from margin], (set a) work, be wrought, **worshipper**.

Righteousness - from <H6663> (tsadaq); **rightness** (abstract), subjective (**rectitude, uprightness as a consequence of being honorable and honest**), objective (justice), moral (virtue) or figurative (**prosperity**) :- justice, moderately, right (-eous) (act, -ly, -ness); a primitive root; to be (causative **make) right** (in a moral or forensic sense) :- cleanse, clear self, (be, do) just (-ice, -ify, -ify self), (be, turn to) righteous (-ness).

Saith - from <H5001> (na'am); **an oracle** :- (hath) said, saith; a primitive root; properly **to whisper**, i.e. (by implication) **to utter as an oracle (a prophesy)** :- say.

CONCLUSION

You may choose to get the wisdom of God's process of thought a little deeper in you understanding. To do this daily confession is one of the best tools I know. I have personalized these so that you can speak these as yours, if not you can just go to your Bible and speak the words as they are written aloud.

This is how this would look as my daily confession:

Isaiah 54:1-17 (KJV)

[1] I Sing, as one who was barren, and did not bear; I break forth into singing, and cry aloud, because although I didn't travail with child: more *are* my children than the children of the married wife, the LORD has declared this. I can take this to the bank.

[2] I enlarge the place of my tent, and stretch forth the curtains of my habitations: I spare not, lengthening my cords, and strengthening my stakes;

[3] For I will break forth on the right hand and on the left; and my seed will inherit the nations, and make the desolate cities to be inhabited.

[4] I Fear not; because I shalt not be ashamed: neither will I be confused or confounded; I will not be put to shame: for I will forget the shame of my youth, and will not remember the reproach of my widowhood any more.

[5] For my Maker *is* my husband; the LORD of hosts *is* his name; and my Redeemer the Holy One of Israel; The God of the whole earth He is called.

[6] For the LORD had called me as a woman forsaken and grieved in spirit, and a wife of youth, when I was refused, said my God.

[7] For a small moment You refused me; but with great mercies You gathered me in.

[8] In a little wrath You hid your face from me for a moment; but with everlasting kindness You will have mercy on me, you are the LORD my Redeemer.

[9] For this *is as* the waters of Noah unto you: for *as* You have

sworn that the waters of Noah should no more go over the earth; so have You sworn that You would not be wroth with me, nor rebuke me.

[10] For the mountains will depart, and the hills be removed; but your kindness shall not depart from me, neither will the covenant of your peace be removed, you are the LORD who has mercy on me.

[11] I was afflicted, tossed with tempest, *and* not comforted, behold, You will lay my stones with fair colors, and lay my foundations with sapphires.

[12] And You will make my windows of agates, and my gates of carbuncles, and all my borders of pleasant stones.

[13] And all my children *are* taught of the LORD; and great *is* the peace of my children.

[14] In righteousness I am established: I am far from oppression; for I will not fear: and from terror; for it will not come near me.

[15] Behold, they will surely gather together, *but* not by You: whosoever shall gather together against me will fall for my sake.

[16] Behold, You have created the smith that blows the coals in the fire, and that brings forth an instrument for his work; and You have created the waster to destroy.

[17] No weapon that is formed against me will prosper; and every tongue *that* rises against me in judgment I shalt condemn. This *is* my heritage as a servant of the LORD, and my righteousness *is* of You, because you, the LORD, said so.

Tarshish Productions

1933 N Stone Maple Ln

Elkhart, Indiana 47514

www.lindacnewberry.com

Info@lindacnewberry.com

www.ingramcontent.com/pod-product-compliance
Lightning Source LLC
Chambersburg PA
CBHW072026040426
42447CB00009B/1757